The History of Jamaica

The
History of
Jamaica

CLINTON V. BLACK F.S.A.

Longman Caribbean

Acknowledgements
The Publishers would like to thank the following for permission to reproduce photographs and prints: BBC Hulton Picture Library, pp. 65, 91, 109; Anne Bolt, p. 76; Mary Evans Picture Library, pp. 26, 34, 38, 56, 73, 79, 81, 86, 99, 100, 101, 106, 113, 128; Institute of Jamaica, pp. 21, 44, 49, 51, 53, 58, 60, 69, 70, 71, 92, 95, 97, 105, 126, 127; Jamaica Archives, pp. 39, 154; Jamaica High Commission, p. 161; Jamaica Information Services, pp. 139, 157, 166, 169; Jamaica Tourist Board, pp. 11, 16, 160, 163; National Maritime Museum, pp. 82, 83; Peter Newark's Western Americana, p. 13; Royal Commonwealth Society, pp. 67, 151, 152, 158; John Topham Picture Library, p. 146; The Zoological Society of London, p. 14.

The cover pictures are reproduced by permission of: The Institute of Jamaica, The Royal Commonwealth Society and The National Maritime Museum.

Maps by Jillian Luff.

Longman Group Limited,
Longman House, Burnt Mill, Harlow
Essex CM20 2JE, England
and Associated Companies throughout the world

Carlong Publishers Caribbean Limited,
P O Box 489
Kingston 10

33 Second Street
Newport West
Kingston 13
Jamaica

Longman Trinidad Limited
Boundary Road
San Juan
Trinidad

First published by Collins Educational 1958
This edition published by Longman Group UK Ltd 1991
Tenth impression 1994

Produced through Longman Malaysia, CL

ISBN 0 582 03898 7

Contents

Important dates in the island's history

1494   Columbus discovered Jamaica and landed (4 May) at Dry Harbour, now called Discovery Bay.

1509   Juan de Esquivel took possession of Jamaica, as first Spanish Governor, for Columbus's son Diego.

1510   Sevilla la Nueva founded.

1534   Spanish Town (Villa de la Vega) founded; Sevilla abandoned.

1655   English expedition under General R. Venables and Admiral W. Penn landed (10 May); the Spaniards capitulated (11 May).

1660   The Spaniards finally expelled from Jamaica.

1670   Jamaica ceded to England by the Treaty of Madrid (8 July).

1692   Earthquake destroyed Port Royal (7 June).

1694   French force under Jean du Casse attacked the island and was defeated at Carlisle Bay (23 July).

1738–9   Treaty of Peace with the Maroons signed.

1760   Formidable slave revolt in St Mary led by Tacky.

1782   Jamaica saved from capture by Admiral Rodney's victory over the French fleet at the Battle of the Saints (12 April).

1795–6   Second Maroon War.

1807   African slave trade in British Colonies abolished (25 March).

1831   Great slave revolt in St James (28 December).

1834   Abolition of slavery and establishment of Apprenticeship system (1 August).

1838   Total abolition of slavery (1 August).

1865   Morant Bay Rebellion (11 October), George W. Gordon hanged.

1866   Crown Colony government adopted.

1868   Banana trade started.

1872   The capital removed from Spanish Town to Kingston.

1884   New Constitution providing for semi-representative government.

1907   Earthquake destroyed Kingston (14 January).

1938   Labour disorders throughout the island. Out of them came the first lasting Labour organisations, and the formation of political parties linked with the unions.

1944   New Constitution – ministerial government (20 November).

1947   First conference on Federation of the British West Indies held at Montego Bay.

1948   University College of the West Indies founded at Mona.

1957   Inauguration of internal self-government (11 November).

1958   Inauguration of Federal Parliament of the West Indies in Port-of-Spain, Trinidad (22 April).

1961   Referendum on Federation held (19 September). Jamaica votes to withdraw.

1962   General Election held (10 April). The Jamaica Labour Party victorious.

1962	Jamaica achieves Independence (6 August) with Sir Alexander Bustamante as first Prime Minister and Sir Kenneth Blackburne as first Governor-General.
	Sir Clifford Campbell, a Jamaican, succeeds Sir Kenneth Blackburne (1 December).
1963	Five-Year Development Plan went to Parliament (July).
1967	Bustamante retired, was succeeded by Donald Sangster whose sudden death brought Hugh Shearer to power.
1969	Norman Manley died (2 September).
1972	General elections held. The People's National Party, led by Michael Manley, won 37 seats to the J.L.P.'s 16.
1976	People's National Party returned to power in the general elections and opts for 'democratic socialism'.
1980	General elections held. The Jamaica Labour Party scores overwhelming victory (October).

Chapter 1

The first Jamaicans

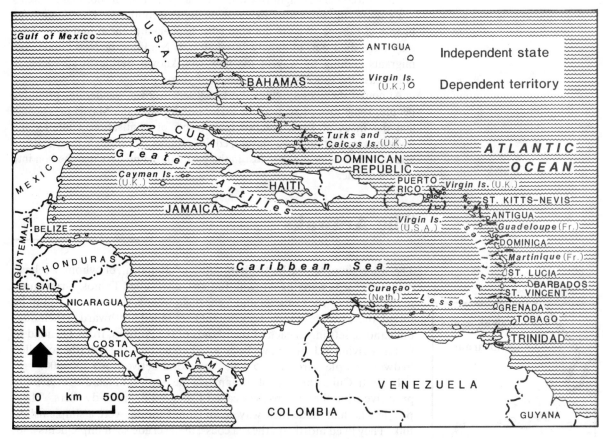

Jamaica and its near neighbours in the Caribbean

The world of which Jamaica is a part is spoken of as *New* because it was discovered by Europeans less than 500 years ago. But the area is as old as the earth itself, and its past reaches as far back in time. The modern or recorded history of Jamaica, as of the other places in this region, is in fact the story of the impact, the effect, upon this old New World of new people and new ideas brought here from the Old World of Europe by the discoverer, Christopher Columbus, and those who followed after him. One of the first results of this impact was the extermination of the first Jamaicans.

The earliest peoples

Although opinions differ, there is a strongly held belief that the earliest people to penetrate into the New World did so between 15 000 and 20 000 years ago. There are various theories as to the way they came. One is that they crossed the Pacific Ocean from island to island and entered by way of Central America. It is now generally believed that they had wandered out of Siberia and across the Bering Strait to Alaska, perhaps on the ice in winter, perhaps on a land bridge when the level of the sea was lower than it is now, perhaps even by boat. They spread slowly southward and, as we know from the stone arrowheads and spear points they left behind, occupied the whole hemisphere.

The newcomers brought fire with them as well as their tool-making skills – a culture, in fact, rather like that of the Palaeolithic or Late Stone Age people of Europe. We are not sure what happened to these first men. They may have died out, or slowly blended with Neolithic or New Stone Age migrants coming by way of the now well-known Bering Strait route. In either case the process took thousands of years.

Although these early New World settlers were a wandering, primitive people, some groups such as the Aztecs of Mexico, the Mayas of Yucatán and the Incas of Peru, reached high levels of civilisation. Cultures and traditions appear to have developed independently through thousands of years. Details of change are lost in the past, but the process marched on into recorded time.

The Arawaks

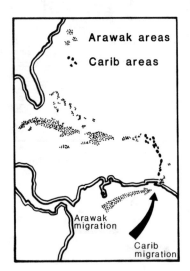

Map showing extent of Arawak areas

The aborigines, or earliest inhabitants, of Jamaica, of whom we have definite records were the Arawak Indians, also called Tainos. Originating in the region of the Guianas and Venezuela where Arawaks are still to be found, these people at some very distant time sailed northward in their dug-out canoes, settling in each of the islands of the Antilles, from Trinidad to Cuba, arriving in Jamaica, we believe, in two waves – the first (the so-called 'redware people') around AD 650, the second between AD 850–900.

In Haiti, Cuba and possibly in Jamaica the Arawaks found an even more primitive tribe than themselves called Ciboneys or 'rock-dwellers.' These people who had made their way down from Florida, were a simple fisher-folk. They lived mostly on the sea coast, made crude shell implements and, it is said, were used as servants by the Arawaks. Our knowledge of the Ciboneys is very scanty. We do not know when they ceased to exist in Jamaica, if indeed they were here. So far no Ciboney sites have been confirmed on the island. Nor are we certain when the calm and peaceful life of the Arawaks was rudely disturbed by the appearance of the fierce man-eating Caribs.[1]

[1] From *Carib* comes, by way of Spanish, the word *cannibal*, an eater of human flesh.

Probably originating in the Guiana region of South America also, this warlike tribe began to spread, as the Arawaks had done, through the islands in their war canoes, leaving death and misery behind them, slaughtering the men and abducting the women. Farther and farther north they swarmed until by the time Columbus discovered the West Indies in 1492 they had taken the whole of the Lesser Antilles and were making frequent raids on the eastern end of Puerto Rico. They were well known and feared in Haiti and from time to time made murderous attacks even on Jamaica. But for the arrival of the Spaniards in the New World, the Caribs might have exterminated these first Jamaicans. As it was, the newcomers from Europe were in a fairly short time to complete the work of destruction.

We do not know as much about these aborigines of Jamaica as we would like. They had no form of writing and so left no written record. A certain amount of information is contained in the books about the area by early Spanish visitors, beginning with Columbus himself, who in his account of his first voyage of discovery, gives a vivid description of his meeting with the Arawak Indians and of all that was new and striking to European eyes. A good deal of evidence was left by the Indians, of course, in the form of refuse heaps, or 'middens' as they are called, in pottery remains, stone implements, wood, stone and rock-carvings, idols and ornaments, even in their own skeletons. From careful study of these remains much information has come to light and investigators trained in this kind of work are still adding to our knowledge.

The Arawaks wore ornaments made of materials such as stone, bone, shell and clay. Above are stone ornaments.

Jamaica appears to have been one of the best settled islands in the Antilles at the time of its discovery in 1494. Remains left by the aborigines show that they lived all over the island, from Priestman's River in the east to Negril in the west; even as far inland as Ewarton and Moneague, as well as in such upland areas as the Long Mountain, and Jack's Hill, 600 metres above the sea – possibly the highest village site in the West Indies. The majority of the villages, however, were close to the coast, in the neighbourhood of rivers, for the Arawaks were sea-going and lived to a great extent off sea-foods.

An interesting village site and one of the largest and most accessible in the island, is that at White Marl on the Caymanas Estates, near Central Village. The Spanish Town Road now cuts through the site and the whole area has changed greatly since Indian times, but we can imagine nevertheless what it was like in those days. Perched on top of the hill, the village commanded a wide view of the surrounding plain, much of which would then have been cultivated fields and gardens, as to a great extent it is today. Then, however, there were no coconut palms, bananas or canes, for these plants had not yet been introduced into the island. Instead, there were probably cultivations of cassava, maize, sweet potato and possibly arrowroot, while among the fruit trees no doubt growing in the area would have been the starapple, naseberry, cashew and guava. Even the course of the Rio Cobre was different: it flowed at that time at the foot of the White Marl Hill, winding at the base of the mountains and entering the sea by way of the Fresh – now known as the Ferry – River. A storm in 1722 changed the Rio Cobre's course and opened for it a more direct route to the harbour.

The Arawaks have long since vanished from White Marl Hill, but on the hill adjacent to the village site now stands the Arawak Indian Museum, administered by the Institute of Jamaica, where extensive study collections are maintained. Actually it is believed that the end of the village was a tragic and violent one, for human bones have been found mixed up with the refuse, suggesting that the settlement was attacked and its people slaughtered.

The Arawaks were clear brown in colour, short and slightly built but well shaped, with straight coarse black hair, a broad face and flattish wide nose. The Spaniards did not consider them beautiful owing chiefly to their custom of flattening the foreheads of children in infancy by tying boards to the frontal bones. One effect of this was to make that part of the skull so hard that it was proof against primitive weapons and even Spanish swords are said to have been blunted and broken on Arawak skulls.

Mild and peaceful, simple and generous by nature, the Arawaks showed the Spaniards more kindness than they deserved. Columbus found them honest and free with all they had, and after a great deal of trading in Haiti, his son says, 'We lost not the value of a pin.' This is not surprising, for besides their natural generosity the Arawaks regarded theft (which was almost unknown among them) as the greatest of crimes, and a particularly brutal form of punishment was reserved for a thief: he was slowly and mercilessly pierced to death with a pole or pointed stick.

The attitude of the Arawaks towards the Spaniards was influenced also by the fact that they regarded the newcomers at first as gods. Among their prophetic songs was one which told of the day when strangers would come among them covered with clothing and armed with the thunders and lightnings of heaven. In fact, in Puerto Rico this belief that the white man was a god and therefore immortal was only shaken by a grimly amusing experiment. A certain Spaniard named Salzedo while on a journey spent a night with an Arawak chief. On the following day the chief, whose name was Brayau, provided him with Indian guides and he set off again on his journey. Soon they came to a river and one of the Indians took Salzedo on his shoulders to carry him across. In mid-river he pretended to stumble and fall, throwing the Spaniard into the stream. Immediately the other Indians fell upon Salzedo and held him under water until he was drowned. At first they refused to believe that the 'god' was really dead and waited two or three days before hurrying back to Brayau with the news. Even he had to see the rotting corpse for himself before he was satisfied. The story of Salzedo soon spread and encouraged the other chiefs to resist the tyranny of the Spaniards who, they now realised, were merely men like themselves.

The Arawaks wore very little clothing; in fact, the men and unmarried girls usually went naked. Sometimes palm leaves or flowers were used for covering, or a short cotton skirt dyed in bright colours and held up by a fibre waist-band. They liked to decorate themselves with feathers, paint and tattoo marks, and often wore ornaments and necklaces of beads. They also had a curious custom of tying their arms and parts of the legs with cotton bands, so tightly wrapped that often the covered parts of the limbs became very thin.

At the time of the discovery the Indians in the Greater Antilles were found to possess some gold in the form of ornaments. Most of this gold appears to have been produced in Haiti and Puerto Rico, finding its way to the other islands in the course of trade. Jamaica had very little gold and such as there was the Indians collected by a simple method. This was by digging holes at the side of a rapid part of a river. The water flowed through these and left a certain amount of silt which was carefully examined for signs of gold. If any was noted the sands were collected and washed repeatedly in order to separate the metal. Primitive though the method was, the Spaniards seem to have used something very similar in their mining efforts on the banks of the Rio Minho near the Longville Estate in Clarendon. The Arawaks did not value gold very highly and cheerfully handed over their golden ornaments to the Spaniards in exchange for cheap trinkets, beads and the like. Within a few years of their arrival the Spaniards are said to have collected every article of gold in all the islands.

Arawak houses were simple in design and frail in appearance, yet they could stand up to strong winds and even hurricanes. They were small, round huts, consisting usually of a tall centre pole driven into the ground, around which smaller posts were placed in a circle. Between these posts lengths of the wild cane were fixed and tied together with vines, or withes, to form the walls. The cone-shaped roof was thatched with grass and palm leaves. The house of the chief, or *cacique* as he was called, was usually larger than the others and sometimes rectangular in shape. The size of a settlement depended on food supply and so varied greatly. In places single families lived by themselves, while some communities might consist of fifty families or more.

Typical Arawak round house and dugout canoe

Apart from earthen pots and other utensils, the main items of furniture were hammocks and wooden stools. The hammock (*hamac*) was an Indian invention; it was not known in Europe before the discovery of the West Indies. These hammocks were made either of cotton string 'openwork', or of a length of woven cotton cloth, sometimes dyed in bright colours. Jamaica was well known at that period for the cultivation of cotton, and much of the women's time was spent spinning and weaving it. In fact Jamaica supplied hammocks and cotton cloth to Cuba and Haiti for some time after those islands had been occupied by Spain, and the Spaniards themselves had sail-cloth made in Jamaica. Because of this one of the many suggested origins of the name *Jamaica* attempts to link it with the Indian word for hammock and to prove that it means 'land of cotton.' The name Jamaica is of great interest. Some of the early Spanish historians, substituting X for J as they often did, write the name *Xaymaca*, but it also appears in its present form in a work published as early as 1511. Columbus called the island *St Jago* (Santiago), but as with the other islands of the Greater Antilles, the Indian name has survived the Spanish. It is commonly thought that Xaymaca in the Arawak language meant 'land of springs', but since the discoverers do not give the meaning of the name (as they do in the case of various place names in Haiti) it is possible that the meaning had already been forgotten by the Indians themselves.

The Arawaks were small eaters and it is said that the amount of food a Spaniard ate in a day would last an Indian a whole week. As already mentioned, their main foodstuffs, apart from fish and shellfish, were cassava, maize (Indian corn) and fruits of many kinds; they also ate birds, conies (a kind of rodent related to the agouti) which they called *utia*, iguanas, yellow snakes and the manatee, or sea-cow.

For maize planting the ground was first cleared by fire by the men. Then the women took over, each armed with a pointed stick and, hanging from their necks, a bag of grain that had been soaked in water for a day or two. They moved along in a row and at each step made a hole with the stick into which they dropped a few grains, covering them with the foot. The children played their part later on by guarding the growing crop from birds. Cassava, like yams, was cultivated in mounds. It was prepared by scraping the roots and cutting them into small pieces; these were pressed and carefully strained to draw off the poisonous juice, then made into cakes which kept fresh for months. Cassava (as well as maize) was also used in the preparation of intoxicating drinks.

The coney is, apart from bats, the only land mammal native to the island. It still survives in remote areas. The Arawaks hunted conies with the help of their only domestic animal, a breed of small barkless dog called *alcos* which, like the Indians themselves, no longer exists. They had various ways of snaring birds: parrots, for example, were usually caught with a noose, doves with a net. Their most ingenious method was that used for catching waterfowl. On discovering a flock of these birds the hunter would allow a number of dry calabashes to float down to them from some distance upstream, until they grew accustomed to these objects in their midst, then taking to the water himself he would approach the flock, his head covered with a calabash in which small holes had been made through which to see

A relative of the guinea pig, the coney was hunted by the Arawaks for food

and breathe. To the birds this appeared to be merely another harmless object floating near them. When close enough the hunter would seize the waterfowl by their legs, one after another, drawing them swiftly under water and, when drowned, stuffing them in a bag which he carried for the purpose.

The Arawaks regarded iguana meat as very delicious and stewed it carefully over a slow fire of sweet wood. They used salt in cooking and seasoned their food with pepper. Fishing was a very important source of food supply and the middens dotted along the coasts of Jamaica are full of mollusc shells and fish and turtle bones. The Indians used nets made of vegetable fibre, bone and turtle-shell hooks and bone-tipped harpoons. In Jamaica and Cuba they had a peculiar method of fishing with the aid of the *remora* or sucking-fish. On a calm morning the remora was carried out to sea tied to the canoe by a long thin line. On seeing a fish it would dart after it and attach itself firmly by means of its powerful sucker. The remora was then pulled by the fisherman to the side of the canoe and its catch removed. Turtles were sometimes caught in this way and even manatees.

The Arawaks made their dugout canoes from the trunks of cedar or silk cotton trees. The trees were felled with the aid of-fire, then hollowed out, first by charring then by chipping with stone axes and chisels. The canoes had keels and were rowed and steered by paddles. They varied greatly in size. Some were made for one person only, others for forty, fifty or more. Columbus saw one in Jamaica 29 metres long and 2.5 metres wide! The Jamaican canoes were particularly well made, 'carved and painted both bow and stern with ornaments so that their beauty is marvellous'.

Columbus also spoke of the skill of the aborigines in the art of working stones. Their stone axes were well-shaped, smooth and beautifully finished. They vary from 25 millimetres to about 230 millimetres in length. Many have been found on the surface of the ground or dug up in fields in the country parts where they are usually called 'thunderbolts' or 'thunder balls.' Placed in the bottom of water-jars they are believed to keep the water cool.

The Arawaks were a pleasure-loving people and enjoyed dancing, singing, smoking and playing their ball-game. The dances were accompanied by singing and the name *areito* was given to both. Some dances were done by women only, others by men, while on certain occasions, such as the marriage of a cacique, both sexes danced together. The dancers drank a good deal of liquor during the performance and often ended up drunk and disorderly.

Next to dancing the Arawaks liked *batos*, their ball game, best. For this they had a special field attached to the village, with large stones arranged for spectators to sit on and carved stools for the caciques. Players were divided into two teams of almost any number, sometimes twenty or thirty a side, and after the ball was thrown it had to be hit from side to side by some member of each team. We do not know what the Arawaks used for a ball. One of the early Spanish historians says it was made from an elastic black substance produced by boiling the roots of certain trees and herbs. As in ping-pong or tennis, if the ball fell 'dead' a point was scored against the side whose turn it was to strike. The ball could be hit with the head, shoulder, hip or knee, but the hands were not used. Sometimes the men and women played together, at other times they played separately. Often teams from different villages played against each other.

Smoking was a popular Arawak pastime. The word tobacco comes from the name for their pipes: *tabaco*. The plant itself they called *cohiba*; it was cultivated on a large scale. The early Spaniards were astonished to see Indians walking about with what they thought were little fire-brands in their mouths! Later they discovered that these were really tubes of dried tobacco leaves tightly rolled as are cigars now. The Arawaks preferred to smoke by pipe, especially at feasts. These were made of a Y-shaped tube, both branches of which were inserted in the nostrils and the smoke deeply inhaled. This method of smoking soon produced unconsciousness.

Jamaica, like Cuba, was divided into provinces each ruled over by a cacique, who was assisted by village headmen or sub-chiefs. Caciques were allowed to have several wives, but their male subjects were permitted only one each. They were treated with great respect and enjoyed by right the best of the fish or game caught and the choicest foodstuffs grown. Their houses were usually bigger than the others, and contained the family idols. If a cacique were ill and dying he would be strangled as a mark of special favour. Other very sick people were generally abandoned in the bush with a little cassava and water and left to die in their hammocks. The Arawaks usually buried their dead in caves, sometimes placing the head and certain bones of the body in a pottery bowl. Some of the best preserved Arawak skulls and the finest examples of their pottery have been found in caves.

Columbus thought at first that the Arawaks had no religion of their own. This was disproved by closer association with them, but, as it happened, the Spaniards took a long time to find out about the religious beliefs of the Arawaks, and the information that exists relates mainly to the island of Haiti. As the practices and beliefs on the other islands are said to have been similar, however, those of Haiti may be taken as typical.

The Arawaks had a number of myths by which they explained the origin of mankind, of various creatures, the sea and so on. The first humans were believed to have come out of two caves. Originally these caves were watched over by a guardian, but one day he forgot to close them up and the sun escaped, as well as the first human beings. The guardian was turned into stone for his carelessness.

These first men were forbidden to look at the sun and in the myths there are accounts of people being changed into birds and trees for disobeying this rule. There is also the story of certain children, abandoned on a river bank, who were eventually turned into frogs which, since then, are always calling 'Toa, toa', which means 'Mother, mother'. The origin of fishes and of the ocean is told in another strange myth in which a calabash containing bones and water was accidentally overturned.

The Arawaks believed in two supreme gods, male and female, the former being called in Jamaica Yocahuna. In addition to these they worshipped a large number of spirits and images called *zemes*. The name was widely used and could mean the spirits themselves or carved images of them, bones or skulls of the dead, the dead or the spirits of the dead, as well as anything believed to have magic powers. Very few wooden zemes survive, but among

This fine copy of a wooden zeme can be seen at the Institute of Jamaica

them are three remarkable ones found in Jamaica in a cave at Spots in Carpenter's Mountains, Manchester, in 1792. They are now in the British Museum, London, but fine casts of them may be seen in the museum of the Institute of Jamaica.

The Arawaks were encouraged by their priests to believe that some zemes could speak, but a party of Spaniards by chance discovered one such zeme in a cacique's hut which had a speaking tube inside it by means of which the idol's divine messages and orders were delivered. The simple Indians believed that the voice they heard was indeed that of a spirit. The cacique is said to have begged the Spaniards not to tell his people of this deception, as he found it very helpful in controlling them!

Great public festivals were sometimes held in honour of the zemes. The cacique usually fixed the day, then sent out messengers to announce it. At the appointed time all the people assembled in their finest dress, the men painted red, yellow and black and wearing bright feather cloaks and headdresses. All had shell ornaments on their arms and legs, which rattled as they moved. The cacique led the parade, playing on a wooden gong. There was singing and dancing, then the ceremony of offering gifts of bread to the zeme. This was later distributed by the priests to the people present, who preserved it until the next festival as a charm against fire and hurricane.

The priests were also the medicine men of the tribe for, as with most primitive peoples, sickness and health were regarded as gifts of the gods. Religious and medicinal knowledge was preserved in certain old songs of which the priests were the guardians. They knew a good deal about the medical value of herbs and some of their cures were real and lasting, but they also used trickery in treating their patients. Sickness was said to be caused by a zeme whom the sick person had offended and who in his anger had placed some foreign substance in the sufferer's body. To cure such cases the priest performed certain ceremonies including the use of tobacco, and ending with his sucking from the affected part of his patient some object which he declared to have been the cause of the trouble. This was usually a pebble or small bone which, of course, he had hidden in his mouth beforehand.

The Arawaks believed that man had a soul which, after death, went to a kind of heaven called *coyaba* – a place of ease and rest where there were no droughts, hurricanes or sickness, and where the time was passed in feasting and dancing. The Carib religion appears in the main to have been very similar to that of the Arawaks. It is interesting to note that the deadly enmity between the two people showed itself even in their religion. The Caribs believed that the souls of brave warriors went to a kind of heaven on certain beautiful, pleasant islands where they were always served by Arawak slaves, but that the souls of cowards went to a desert land beyond a high mountain where they themselves became the slaves of Arawak masters!

Chapter 2

The discovery of Jamaica

Such, then, were the first Jamaicans – a peaceful, primitive people, still in the Stone Age stage of development as the fifteenth century AD drew to its close. Meanwhile across the Atlantic, the vast and unknown ocean that lay between the New World and the Old, civilised man in Europe was even then entering a new and wonderful era of development later to be known as the Renaissance, or the Rebirth of Learning.

Starting in Italy, this great revival, which marks the end of the Middle Ages and the beginning of modern Europe, was spreading westward over the Continent by the close of the fifteenth century. It affected every aspect of the arts, every branch of science. In Spain and Portugal the main energies were directed towards the development of navigation, by advances in astronomy and a new interest in map-making.

Christopher Columbus

One of the most outstanding products of the age was Christopher Columbus, the man who was to discover the New World for the Old. Born in Genoa, Italy, in 1451, Columbus was the son of a wool weaver and followed this trade for a time. Seafaring was the calling which appealed to him most, however, and besides making maps and charts for a living, he took part in voyages of one kind or another from an early age. He is said to have accompanied a Portuguese expedition to the Gold Coast, West Africa, in 1481–82.[1]

Gradually the idea came to him that much of the world probably remained undiscovered, and he devised his 'Enterprise of the Indies' as he called it – a plan for reaching Asia by sailing westward. The enterprise had three main motives: the need for a new route to China and the East to

[1] First settled by Portuguese, the Gold Coast in time attracted adventurers and traders from almost every European nation. It became a British colony in the second half of the nineteenth century and is now the independent state of Ghana.

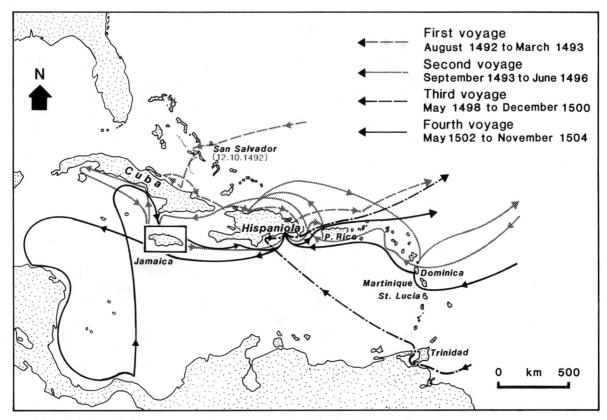

First voyage
August 1492 to March 1493

Second voyage
September 1493 to June 1496

Third voyage
May 1498 to December 1500

Fourth voyage
May 1502 to November 1504

The routes of Columbus's four voyages in the Caribbean

replace the old one through the Levant and Middle East; the desire to spread the Christian faith to distant lands; and the thirst for geographical knowledge, for gold and adventure.

For many disheartening years Columbus tried to interest various European governments in his idea, without success. At length in 1492 he made an agreement with the Spanish sovereigns, Ferdinand and Isabella, which provided that he was to command an expedition fitted out mainly at the Crown's expense, 'to discover and acquire islands and mainland in the Ocean Sea'. Among the rewards which he demanded was the title of Admiral, the Vice-royalty of all territories discovered and a tenth of all the gold, silver, gems, spices and other merchandise resulting either from conquest or trade.

The first voyage

On 3 August 1492, Columbus in his flagship the *Santa Maria*, accompanied by two caravels the *Niña* and *Pinta*, with crews totalling ninety men and, boys, sailed from Palos de la Frontera, in Spain, on his great voyage of discovery. On 12 October he landed on one of the Bahamas, the *Guanahani* of the Indians, now known as Watling Island, but which Columbus named San Salvador (Holy Saviour) in thanksgiving to the Lord

Columbus's exploration of Jamaica

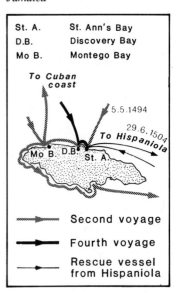

St. A.   St. Ann's Bay
D.B.   Discovery Bay
Mo B.   Montego Bay

To Cuban coast

5.5.1494

29.6.1504
To Hispaniola

Mo B.   D.B.   St. A.

⟶⟶⟶ Second voyage

⟶ Fourth voyage

⟶ Rescue vessel from Hispaniola

who had brought him safely to port. He had arrived in the New World, but did not know it. He remained convinced until his death that, as he had expected to, he had found islands off the coast of eastern Asia, hence the name West Indies. From Amerigo Vespucci, a Florentine navigator and one of Columbus's successors, came the later name *America*.

On his first voyage Columbus explored various islands of the Bahamas, the north east coast of Cuba and part of the north coast of Hispaniola – *La Isla Española* – or Haiti, the Arawak name by which it is called to-day. The *Santa María* ran aground off Hispaniola and had to be abandoned. A small fort was built out of the material of the stranded vessel and the crew left in charge of it to start a small settlement on the island.

The second voyage

It was on his second voyage, after revisiting Hispaniola and Cuba that Columbus discovered Jamaica. In Hispaniola he found to his dismay that the fort had been destroyed and its occupants slaughtered by the natives in revenge for ill-treatment they had received from the Spaniards. It was from the Indians of Cuba that Columbus learnt of Jamaica. They knew the island's name but wrongly described it as the source of 'the blessed gold'. On the afternoon of 3 May 1494, Columbus in the well-tried little caravel *Niña*, with two others the *San Juan* and the *Cardera*, set a course for Jamaica, arriving on Monday the 5th at what we now know as St Ann's Bay, but which Columbus called *Santa Gloria* 'on account of the extreme beauty of its country'. Columbus thought Jamaica 'the fairest island that eyes have beheld; mountainous and the land seems to touch the sky . . . all full of valleys and fields and plains'.

This part of the island was full of villages, thickly populated with Indians who gave the Admiral a hostile reception as his fleet approached the bay. Sixty or seventy canoes laden with angry shouting warriors put out to meet him and he was forced to scatter them with blank shot. He spent the night anchored off Santa Gloria and the next day sailed down the coast to a harbour 'shaped like a horseshoe' which he named *Puerto Bueno*. Later called Dry Harbour, this is now known as Discovery Bay in memory of the event, although there is a strong belief that the honour belongs to the present Rio Bueno, a few kilometres farther westward.

Here also the Indians were unfriendly, but Columbus was determined to land for he needed wood and water and a chance to repair his vessels. So he sent the ship's boat on ahead with crossbowmen who killed and wounded a number of the Indians. The Spaniards also let loose a big dog on shore which chased the terrified Arawaks and bit several of them savagely. Then Columbus landed and took possession of the island in the name of Ferdinand and Isabella of Spain.

The following day six Indians brought peace offerings of cassava, fruit and fish, and for the rest of the Admiral's stay supplied him and his men regularly with provisions in exchange for trinkets and other trade goods. One thing only disappointed Columbus sorely – the absence of any trace of the gold he had been led to believe he would find in Jamaica. On 9 May the fleet sailed westward to Montego Bay – *El Golfo de Buen Tiempo* as Columbus called it, 'Fair Weather Gulf' – where they took on board an Indian who, in spite of the protests of his wife and children, begged to be allowed to join the Spaniards. The fleet then set sail for Cuba.

From May to July Columbus continued his cruise along the Cuban coast, then crossed over again to Jamaica to complete the exploration of this island. From Montego Bay the fleet sailed round the western end and east along the coast, spending the nights anchored close in, and regularly supplied with food from the Indians who were more friendly here than on the north side. The fleet was troubled by squalls and thunderstorms until the second week of August, when it put in at Portland Bight or, as Columbus called it, *Bahía de la Vaca*, 'Cow Bay', perhaps because of the number of sea-cows that he saw there.

There were many Indian villages near the Bay and here Columbus says he found the most intelligent and civilised aborigines of all he met in the Antilles. Here, too, by means of an interpreter he had a most interesting conversation with the cacique of a large village on a mountain slope who, together with his family and chief followers, paid the Admiral a visit. One of the cacique's men who stood alone on the prow of the canoe, wore a

Indians bringing Columbus peace offerings

cloak of red feathers shaped like a coat of arms, a great crown of feathers and carried a white banner. Most of the other men had their faces painted in various colours, wore feather helmets and large, round forehead ornaments. Two men, painted differently from the rest, carried trumpets made of a very black wood covered with carvings of birds and other designs.

The cacique himself although almost naked, wore many rich ornaments. Around his head was a band of small stones of different colours, but mainly green, evenly arranged with large white ones in between, and connected in front by a big gold ornament.[1] From his ears two golden plates hung from rings made of small green stones, and around his neck were copper ornaments attached to a necklace of white beads.

During their conversation the cacique asked Columbus to take him and his family to Spain. He said he had heard that nobody in the islands could stand up to the Admiral's power and so before he was deprived of his land and his authority as a cacique he wished to see the wonders of Spain. Columbus, however, refused to take them with him. He remained only a day in Portland Bight, then continuing his cruise saw the last of Jamaica at Morant Point as he stretched away once more for Hispaniola.

The fourth voyage

Nine years later, while on his fourth and last voyage, Columbus was to visit Jamaica again, this time in sad and tragic circumstances. It was while on his way back from the American mainland in early May, 1503, that it became clear that his two battered, worm-eaten caravels *Capitana* and *Santiago* were in no state for an Atlantic crossing. He tried to make for Hispaniola but, battered by a storm off the west end of Cuba, ran for Jamaica instead, reaching Discovery Bay on 23 June. The lack of fresh water here forced him to sail eastward to St Ann's Bay where he stranded the ships side by side a bow's shot from the shore. With heavy hearts the Admiral and his company, including his young son Ferdinand and Bartholomew his brother, watched the vessels fill with water and settle for good in the soft sand of the bay. Unable now to use the cabins, the Spaniards were forced to build palm-thatched shelters on the decks of the caravels as protection from sun and rain.

Columbus was fortunate in his choice of a refuge. No better spot for the purpose could have been found on the north coast. He was in a strong position in case of attack from land or sea, two fresh water streams flowed nearby and there was the large Arawak village of Maima about 750 metres away from which to draw provisions. The Indians proved friendly and by arrangement brought fresh supplies of food each day in exchange for cheap ornaments and trade goods. A glass bead or two bought a cake of cassava, and for a hawk's bell the Arawaks would give up their most prized

[1] These metal ornaments were made of an alloy of gold and copper which the Indians called *guanin*. It came by way of the Lesser Antilles from the South American mainland.

possession. Gifts of a pair of scissors or a looking glass were made to the caciques or village headmen from time to time to keep them friendly.

The main problem was how to get off the island. The only answer lay in sending someone to Hispaniola by dugout canoe, since it was impossible to repair the caravels or build another. Columbus called for volunteers for the perilous journey and only Diego Méndez, one of his most faithful followers, came forward. 'I have but one life,' he said, 'and I am willing to sacrifice it in the service of your lordship, and for the welfare of all those who are here with us.' Méndez was later joined by a Genoese, Bartolomé Fieschi. The Admiral's brother accompanied the volunteers and their Indian paddlers to the east end of the island and watched them out of sight before returning to St Ann's Bay and the long wait. As it happened, Méndez and Fieschi made the hard and dangerous journey in safety, but a year was to pass before Columbus knew for certain that they had.

Meanwhile at St Ann's Bay, as the weeks lengthened to months, hopes of rescue grew weaker. Sickness broke out among the ships' company: Columbus himself suffered a severe attack of arthritis. The Spaniards grew fearful, uneasy and their discontent soon turned to open mutiny. Accusing Columbus of wishing to keep them all in Jamaica for good, the mutineers, led by the brothers Francisco and Diego Porras, seized ten dugout canoes which the Admiral had bought, together with all the provisions on hand, and set off eastward along the coast intending to attempt the crossing to Hispaniola as Méndez had done. Along the way they ill-treated and robbed the Indians, telling them to go to Columbus for payment for the supplies they took and to kill him if he refused to pay. Their attempt to reach Hispaniola failed. They ran into bad weather soon after they started and growing fearful of the heavy seas decided to lighten their canoes by throwing the Indian paddlers overboard, chopping off their hands when they attempted to cling to the sides of the boats.

Forced back to land the rebels ran riot through the island, ill-treating the natives and undoing all the good that Columbus's kindness and fair dealing had achieved. At St Ann's Bay the food supply from the Indians began to fall off, 'they being a people who take small pains in cultivation', as Ferdinand Columbus wrote, 'and we consuming more in a day than they ate in twenty'. Besides, the Arawaks had lost interest in the trade for they now had all the trinkets and toys they wanted.

Columbus's position could hardly have been worse. Shipwrecked, painfully sick, deserted by many of his followers, abandoned (for it seemed that help would never come from Hispaniola), he now found himself and his company faced also with starvation. It was not long, however, before he thought of a device which he hoped would solve one difficulty, that of food supplies. Knowing from a book on astronomy he had with him that there would soon be an eclipse of the moon, he decided to play on the fears of the natives for his own benefit. Calling them together he told them that the God he served was angry with them for stopping the supply of food and intended to punish them severely, as a proof of which the moon they loved so much would soon be turned to blood. The Indians did not really believe him at first, but when on the night predicted the moon went into eclipse they were terrified and with loud cries of distress begged him to plead with God on their behalf, promising on their part to furnish all the food the Spaniards might need. Columbus at length agreed to plead for them and when the moon eventually came out of the shadows they were overjoyed and deeply thankful. The device had succeeded and from then on the food supply never failed.

But other trials were in store. Don Nicolás de Ovando, the governor of Hispaniola, hated Columbus and made no effort to provide Diego Méndez with a rescue ship. In fact he added to the Admiral's anguish by sending a small caravel to St Ann's Bay to spy out the position and report back to him, but with instructions not to take off Columbus or his men. The caravel spent less than a day anchored near the grounded vessels, then sailed away, leaving behind as the only supplies after a year of hunger a slab of salt pork and a cask or two of wine.

The visit of the caravel was proof, however, that Méndez and Fieschi had arrived in Hispaniola after all, and gave grounds for hope that help would be forthcoming. This cheering sign did not come a day too soon: it had the effect of checking another revolt which was on the point of breaking out among the Admiral's remaining company.

During this time the Porras brothers and their followers had moved close to St Ann's Bay, and Columbus with characteristic kindness sent them a large slice of the salt pork, and an offer of pardon. This they refused, for they had now decided to attack and capture the stranded vessels if possible. At Maima they were met by the Admiral's brother, Bartholomew, and fifty armed men, who again made them an offer of peace, but they were determined to fight and a small-scale battle took place.

Porras and six of his men went for Bartholomew, thinking that with him dead the rest would be easy, but the brave Bartholomew fought like a lion. He laid three of his enemies low with his first three blows then came to grips with the rebel leader himself. Porras aimed a savage blow at Bartholomew but his sword bit harmlessly into the other's shield and he was quickly overpowered and bound as his followers fled. The following day the surviving rebels surrendered and were freely pardoned by Columbus; he even spared the lives of the Porras brothers, but kept them in custody on board ship.

While these events were taking place, in Hispaniola Diego Méndez was fitting out the rescue vessel. Refused assistance by Ovando, he had had to wait for the arrival of a fleet from Spain before he could charter a small caravel on his own account. Towards the end of June 1504, the little vessel arrived at St Ann's Bay and the desperate year-long wait was at an end. On the 29th she left for Hispaniola with Columbus and the survivors of his crew, about a hundred in all; in September he sailed for Spain. He was never to see the New World again. He died at Valladolid on 20 May 1506. In accordance with a wish which he expressed before his death, his remains were taken from Spain to Hispaniola in 1542 and placed in a vault in the Cathedral of Santo Domingo which is still said to contain the Discoverer's bones.

Chapter 3

Jamaica under the Spaniards

Great explorer and brilliant navigator though he was, Columbus had neither the experience nor ability necessary to be a successful colonial administrator. After his failure with the colony in Hispaniola the Spanish monarchs lost confidence in him. Though they treated him with all courtesy, he was never again allowed to interfere in the government of his island of Hispaniola, or to enjoy the privileges of admiral and viceroy which should have been his under the original agreement made with Ferdinand and Isabella. He died a sad old man, trying to the end to regain his lost privileges.

Diego, his son, who succeeded to his titles, managed to recover some of his rights by means of a lawsuit. He was appointed Governor of the Indies in 1508 and in the following year went out to Hispaniola to take up his post. On arrival, however, he discovered that Jamaica, although a dependency of Hispaniola, had been already given to Diego de Nicuesa and Alonso de Ojeda jointly as a place from which to draw supplies for the mainland. In order to secure his right to the island Columbus appointed Juan de Esquivel governor; he was to be the first of more than twenty Spanish governors who, during nearly a century and a half, were to administer the affairs of Jamaica.

The story of this period was almost unknown until this century. Very few notices of Jamaica are to be found in old Spanish histories, while English information for the period is scanty, being limited largely to the story of the island's conquest. No Spanish records appear to have survived in Jamaica. It was known, however, that a great deal of information about the island probably existed in the archives in Spain, and research there has resulted in the publication of two books[1] from which we get a much clearer picture than was possible before of Jamaica under the Spaniards.

Generally speaking the island as a Spanish colony was a failure from the start. It never prospered, was always poor, and more of a burden than a

[1] *Jamaica Under the Spaniards* by Frank Cundall & Joseph L. Pietersz. Kingston, Jamaica, 1919; and *Jamaica Española* by Francisco Morales Padrón. Seville, Spain, 1952.

benefit to Spain. As early as 1512 there was a move to withdraw the colonists and send them to Cuba. Interest in the island soon faded when it became clear there was no gold to be found, but not before a large number of Indians had been worked to death in the search for the precious metal.

The destruction of the Arawaks

A terrible blot oh the period of Spanish rule in Jamaica (as elsewhere in the West Indies), was the extermination of the aboriginal inhabitants, the Arawak Indians. Horrifying accounts of Spanish brutality to these gentle people are given by historians of the period. In Hispaniola it is reported that the settlers frequently murdered Indians in sport, to keep their hands in use, laying bets among themselves to see who could most expertly strike off an Indian's head at a blow.

A system had been set up in the islands by which large grants of land were made to settlers who were permitted to compel the native Indians to work for them. The system was shockingly abused, the Indians were over-worked, ill-treated and ill-fed. Vast numbers died as a result and thousands more committed suicide by hanging themselves or drinking poisonous cassava juice to escape from their bondage. Mothers are said to have

A great number of Indians died under Spanish rule, many of them tortured to death

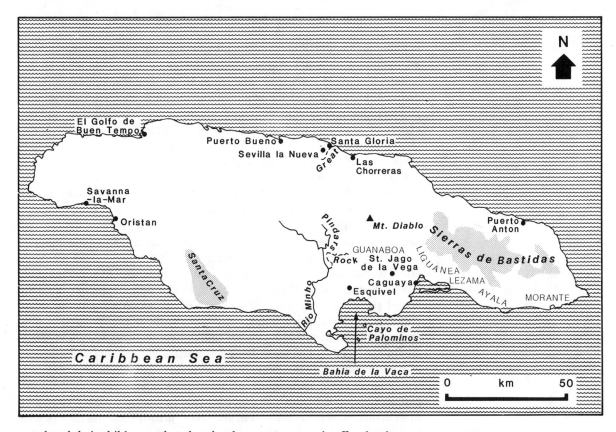

Spanish Jamaica

murdered their children rather than let them grow up and suffer the slavery they had known.

A great many Arawaks must also have died from European diseases, especially smallpox, to which they would have had little resistance. We know that in Jamaica, for instance, in 1520 there was a 'general pestilence . . . among the Indians' which killed off a large number. Other destructive enemies were the animals introduced by the Spaniards – the pigs, goats and cattle – which multiplied rapidly and in time roamed wild, destroying the unfenced Arawak cultivations, rooting up their cassava and trampling and grazing their corn.

In 1598 the Governor of Jamaica, Fernando Melgarejo, alarmed at the speed at which the Indian population was dwindling, proposed that a special area be reserved for them in which to live and have their cultivations. The Indians naturally welcomed the suggestion, but the colonists objected to it on the ground that they would be deprived of the services of the Indians. So failed the last effort to save the first Jamaicans. By 1655 when the English captured the island – and probably for some time before – they had been completely wiped out.

Spanish settlement

Jamaica's main use to Spain was as a supply base. In the early days of colonisation men, horses, arms and food from here helped in the conquest of Cuba and much of the American mainland, but after that the island's importance grew less and less. Almost nothing was done to develop the country's natural resources. The chief trade was the supply of fresh provisions to passing ships (for Jamaica lay on the route from Cartagena to Havana: that taken by the treasure fleets on their homeward trip), and the export of hides and lard to Havana and the mainland. In exchange, the ships that touched here brought the colonists supplies of clothing, wine, oil, wheaten flour and a few luxury articles.

Vast herds of swine roamed the rich grazing areas of St Ann and the western parishes, and great numbers of these animals were killed each year for the sake of their fat. There was an annual slaughter of cattle also 'only to get the hides and the fat, leaving the meat wasted,' while from the skins of the goats which ran wild in the mountains excellent leather was made.

The Spaniards introduced a number of fruit trees and food plants in order to increase their food supply, and to them the West Indies owe, amongst other foods, the banana, plantain and all the varieties of citrus except the grapefruit. They grew sugar in Jamaica for local use only, grinding it in horse-driven mills; cultivated cotton, cocoa, tobacco as well as the grapevine from which they are said to have made a good claret. They also brewed a kind of pimento drink described as 'a very wholesome liquor, and more beneficial than brandy.'

In spite of these activities, the Jamaica settlers were poor for the most part and harassed by the high cost of living. Few people wished to go out from Spain and settle in the island, and many already there did their best to leave. Stories of large quantities of silver and gold coins having been buried in Jamaica by the Spaniards are probably quite untrue. Throughout the occupation the only coins in use appear to have been copper ones. In fact in 1644 there was so much copper currency in the island of so little and unfixed a value that it was suggested that the King should order a careful account to be taken of what there was; and half of it to be melted and used for making cauldrons, sugar boilers and other articles. When the Spaniards withdrew from Jamaica at the coming of the English, they fully believed that in time they would retake the island; so they buried their copper money and drew up an official list of the hiding places with special marks in order to show clearly each separate claim. Edward Long in his *History of Jamaica*, published in 1774, says that 'large quantities of [these coins] . . . have been dug up in Spanish Town, the hills adjacent to it, and other parts; but no gold nor silver coin was ever found, that I have heard of.'

No doubt Columbus's connections with Santa Gloria (St Ann's Bay) played a part in its choice as the site of the first Spanish settlement on the island. They called it *Sevilla la Nueva*, New Seville. Among the first settlers were some of the sailors who had been stranded there with the Discoverer six years before. The town was founded by Esquivel in 1510 on Diego Columbus's order, near the site of the old Arawak village of Maima. It would have been of some size had the original plan been carried out. Among the larger structures were a fort, a fortified castle, and a church which was never finished. But *Sevilla* was not a success, chiefly because of its unhealthy position close to swamps. In twenty years the settlers did not manage to rear ten children, although many had been born. So the place was abandoned fourteen years after its foundation by order of the King of Spain, and its people moved to the south side of the island and settled on the site which became the *Villa de la Vega*, better known as *St Jago de la Vega*, and now as Spanish Town.

Of New Seville little or nothing remains today, except a well, what may be a fragment of the old fort, and some foundations scattered over the canefields of Seville Estate, as the place became. In 1937 a number of carved stones – possibly some of those which were to have been built into the castle – were discovered in the well; others were found buried in the ground near by. They consist of half-columns, the side posts of doorways, panels and the like, all finely carved with figures of various creatures, fruits and foliage. These stones, together with others since found buried on the site, represent some of the earliest artistic efforts of Europeans in the New World, and are our chief relics of Spanish Jamaica. Most of them are in the museum of the Institute. On 17 November 1982, the Inter-American Council for Education Service and Culture formally declared New Seville an historic site of the Americas. The Jamaica government has planned there for 1992 the creation of a monumental historical and archaeological park which will be presented as part of the commemoration of the 500th anniversary of the arrival of Christopher Columbus in the New World.

Settlements and townships established by the Spaniards, besides those already mentioned, included that at *Caguaya* (Passage Fort), *Esquivel* (Old Harbour, named for the first governor), *Oristan* (Bluefields), *Las Chorreras* (near Ocho Rios), Savanna-la-Mar and *Puerto Antón* (Port Antonio). The Spaniards used the low-lying lands for their *hatos* or cattle ranches, chief among which was that of *Morante* (the name lingers in Morant Bay), *Ayala* (the present Yallahs), *Lezama* (where Mona now is), *Liguanea* (in Lower St Andrew) and *Guanaboa* (in St Catherine). Other important *hatos* were located near Old Harbour, in Vere, on the Pedro Plains, behind Bluefields and near Savanna-la-Mar. Of the roads in Spanish times, few were better than bridle paths. The two main trails were, one along the south coast, and another which crossed the island from the mouth of the St Ann's Great River over the Golden Spring Gap to Alderton, thence near the site of the present village of Kellits, down the Pindars River, the Rock River, the Rio Minho and the Palmetto Gully to the St Catherine Plain, keeping for much of the way to the river beds. Many of the rivers bear their Spanish names, but only two mountain ranges still do, that of *Santa Cruz* and *Mount Diablo*. The Blue Mountains were called *Sierras de Bastidas*.

Spanish Town early became the centre of activity. It is sometimes said that Diego Columbus probably laid the foundations, but he had died some years before the royal decree for the establishment of the town was issued. His son, Don Luis, became the third admiral in the Columbus family but he was not granted the title of viceroy. Like his father, he brought a lawsuit against the Crown to recover his rights, but in the end agreed to give up all claims in return for a grant of the province of Veragua in Central America and the island of Jamaica, with the titles Duke of Veragua and Marquis de la Vega (this latter being so called after the capital of the island). The Marquises continued to enjoy these rights until 1640, when the Crown took over full control of Jamaica.

Besides its convenient and healthful situation, with an ample water supply and fertile country round about, Spanish Town enjoyed protection from direct sea attack, while being sufficiently near to two good harbours. There are a number of interesting accounts of the town written during the Spanish occupation. A Carmelite missionary, Antonio Vázquez de Espinosa, writing around 1628, says the site was 'marvellously attractive . . . very well built and laid out.' An unwelcome English visitor, Captain William Jackson, who plundered Spanish Town fifteen years later, thought it a fair town, consisting of four or five hundred houses, five or six stately churches and chapels, and one monastery of Franciscan friars. The people of the town had had warning of Jackson's approach and took to the hills with most of their valuables. The place was held to ransom, nevertheless. Meanwhile the invaders enjoyed a pleasing change from ship food and, we are told, feasted on 'Hoggs, Henns and other good provisions.'

Unfortunately no Spanish buildings now exist. In 1761 the Hall of Audience, which stood in the Spanish Town Square, was pulled down to make way for the King's House (now itself a ruin); so, too, was the old Spanish tavern which is said to have been, up to the end of the eighteenth century, on the site of the present Rodney Memorial. Although most of the houses were of wood and tiles, some were built of brick. They were usually one storey in height, built low for fear of earthquakes and hurricanes.

Although strictly speaking the island was under the control of Spain, it was to some extent self-governing. The governors were usually appointed by the Duke of Veragua and governed with the aid of the *cabildo*, a council of nominated members. If the governor were strong he governed largely by himself; if weak, the *cabildo* ruled; if tactless, he ran into trouble with the church authorities.

The church played an important part in the life of the times. There is still a Red Church and a White Church Street in Spanish Town, both named for Spanish chapels, as well as a Monk Street – a reminder of the dark-robed, sandalled figures which were once a familiar feature of the old town. In 1581 Francisco Márquez de Villalobos was the first abbot to live in Jamaica. 'Previous Abbots,' he wrote, 'had had more concern in making incomes than in attending to their duties.' He died twenty-five years later and was buried near the high altar of the principal church in Spanish Town. It was the abbots of Jamaica who sent back to Spain the descriptive accounts of the island which are of so much interest and value to us today.

Life on the whole was rather difficult and often dull in Spanish Jamaica. The people were poor (although one abbot blamed this on their own laziness) and on at least one occasion had nothing but cassava and beef to eat. Epidemics broke out from time to time, and some years brought with them earthquakes, hurricanes and droughts. In spite of the charge of laziness the colonists must have spent some time and effort in cultivating, cattle rearing and other useful activities. We know from the records that they kept shops, had a number of tanneries and did a certain amount of shipbuilding for which there was an abundance of good timber, especially cedar and mahogany. They made cloth from the cotton grown on the island, dyeing it with Brazil-wood and other dyes.

Life had its lighter side as well. There were dances, ball games and tournaments of various kinds; there were the regular feast-day celebrations, at least one of which – that of St John – combined pleasure with profit. On that day the people went out to the *Cayo de Palominos*, Pigeon Island, to celebrate. At that time of the year the cay was usually so full of young doves that those who went out not only cooked and ate as many as they could, but loaded their boats with the young birds for the return journey.

The community remained a small one with the usual result that people tended to meddle in each other's affairs. This frequently led to quarrels, some of which ended seriously. In 1648, for example, Pedro de Valbuena, a Franciscan monk, preached a sermon condemning card playing as sinful, especially by people in authority. The governor, Pedro de Caballero, who knew full well that the monk was referring to him, called Valbuena a liar and an immoral monk! Caballero who, we are told, was thirty years old at the time, of medium build, black-bearded and freckled, appears to have been a troublemaker. Some time before he had called the abbot, Medina Moreno, 'a garlick-eating clown,' for which the abbot had excommunicated him. Jacinto Sedeño de Albornoz (who had recently come out to audit the accounts), took a hand in this quarrel that became out of control, caused a good deal of public disorder, and ended in the death of Caballero during a scuffle and the arrest of both Sedeño and the abbot.

In the last years of the Spanish occupation the colony had been weakened by internal strife of this kind. The Duke of Veragua failed to support his governors or to keep order. The governors on their part quarrelled with the church authorities, and in the twelve years before the English conquest, one governor, Francisco Ladrón de Zegama, died a prisoner in his own house; another, Caballero, died by violence as we have seen, and Sedeño his successor, was deprived of his office after a riot and sent away to prison.

But there were other sources of internal division. With the joining of Portugal to the Spanish Crown in 1580, a number of Portuguese families emigrated to Jamaica, including some Jews who were to form the nucleus of the present Jewish community. The old settlers did not get along well with the newcomers, however, with the result that some Spaniards emigrated to Cuba while a number of Portuguese were expelled from Jamaica.

Threats to Spanish rule

Another corrupting influence in the colony came from the frequent attacks by pirates. These attacks were by no means limited to Jamaica, but formed part of a general effort by certain European nations to loosen Spain's grip on the area. On the discovery of the New World by Columbus, the Pope had issued proclamations dividing the Indies between Spain and Portugal, but it was not long before other European nations began to challenge the justice of this division. 'I should like', declared Francis I, King of France, 'to see the clause of Adam's will that excludes me from a share of the world'. So, national rivalries in Europe spread to distant lands, and from the mid-

1500s to the end of the eighteenth century the rich countries of the Caribbean were the scene of international naval and commercial competition, the story of which is closely linked with the general history of Europe.

As early as 1506 French ships appeared in the Caribbean, attacking small Spanish settlements and capturing Spanish vessels. By 1542 the Dutch were already trading in these waters. The English came late into the region; although ships under Sebastian Cabot[1] visited the Brazilian coast in 1516 it was not until John Hawkins made his three famous voyages some forty or fifty years later that England began to make a serious effort to break down Spain's control of the trade of the New World. One of the early effects of this international rivalry was the appearance of pirate craft off Jamaica's coasts.

As early as 1555 the colonists had to chase away two French ships. During the next hundred years other Frenchmen were to come, as well as Dutch, Italian, Portuguese and English, all prepared to trade, or to plunder. Although it was illegal some of the colonists traded secretly with the pirates, but these outsiders did not always come to trade. In 1597, for example, Sir Anthony Shirley landed, and meeting with little resistance plundered the island. He marched on Spanish Town, guided there by an Arawak Indian, and easily sacked and burnt the town. He and his companions found Jamaica 'a marvellous fertile isle', more pleasant and wholesome than any other they had visited. In a report sent from Jamaica to Spain in 1644, it is stated that these raids made the settlers 'so nervous and terrified that if two ships are seen off the port, without waiting to know where they are from, they remove the women and their effects to the mountains. The time they waste in doing this gives the enemy the opportunity to return and occupy the town without resistance.'

Fernando Melgarejo, who became Governor in 1597, was very active against these pirates and hunted them from one end of the island to the other. He lived in fear of the sworn vengeance of a French pirate named Olibos whose brother Melgarejo had killed while beating off an attack. But Melgarejo's greatest action was his defeat of Christopher Newport in 1603 when the latter tried to invade the island with an armed force far outnumbering that of the Spanish defenders. Newport himself admitted that the governor had fought like 'a good knight' and later congratulated him and his soldiers. In his report to Spain Melgarejo said that victory was won not so much by strength of arms as by a miracle. Indeed, a Spanish writer of the period says that the English later declared that the chief cause of their defeat was a friar, mounted on a powerful horse and singing the hymn of victory. This figure was identified with St James, patron saint of Spain, on the eve of whose festival the battle had taken place. 'Accordingly', says the same writer, 'from that time on the town sends its prayers to him and has him as their patron; on his day they hold a fiesta there and a general celebration in commemoration of this victory'.

In spite of Melgarejo's efforts, his successor Alonso de Miranda found the island infested with pirates, including a well-known Portuguese named

[1] Cabot discovered North America in 1497.

Mota, who went along the whole coast sacking and plundering the ranches and carrying off the inhabitants.

Up to the end of the sixteenth century the only settled colonies in the West Indies were those of Spain. So far the challenge by other European nations of Spanish claims in the area had taken the form of raiding and smuggling. The first English experiments in colonisation started at the beginning of the seventeenth century, in Virginia (North America), Bermuda (by accident of shipwreck), and Guiana, but it was not until 1624 that the first permanent English settlement in the West Indies was started, by Thomas Warner in St Kitts. This was followed by the settling of Barbados three years later, of Nevis in 1628, and of Antigua and Montserrat in 1632.

In 1643 Captain William Jackson with a force of over a thousand men landed at Passage Fort. He marched on Spanish Town, as already mentioned, and plundered it. His men liked the island so well that many deserted and had to be left behind. These raids were opening the eyes of more and more people to the attractions and strategic value of the island.

Down from the hills came the people of Spanish Town as Jackson's fleet sailed away, and soon life went on as before in the town. But a violent change was coming for these Spanish colonists. On 10 May 1655, another English fleet appeared off Kingston Harbour (as it is now called) and the townspeople prepared to move once more to the mountains. Another raid, they thought, as they packed their valuables for flight – but this time they were wrong. As the fleet drew nearer, so did the end of Spanish rule in Jamaica.

Chapter 4

The coming of the English

The fleet that sailed into Kingston Harbour in May 1655, had been sent out by Oliver Cromwell as part of a plan (known as the 'Western Design') aimed against Spain. In England religious difficulties and friction between the King and Parliament had resulted in the outbreak of civil war in 1642. On the execution of King Charles I, the country became a Commonwealth with Cromwell as Lord Protector from 1653 until his death five years later.

The original English colonies in the West Indies were soon brought under the control of Parliament and plans began to be made which were to lead to the capture of Jamaica. For a long time relations between England and Spain had been for the most part those of enemies, and the Western Design had as its general object the taking over of all the vast territories held by Spain in the Caribbean. There was no shortage of motives for this undertaking, among them religious and commercial ones. There were also wrongs to be avenged, including the deportation by the Spanish of the English settlers at St Kitts in 1629, as well as the countless attacks on English ships in West Indian waters and the murder or enslavement of the crews.

Oliver Cromwell, English general and statesman

The Design, if successful, would have been a serious blow to Spain, but, as events were to show, it had been based on the belief that that country was weaker than she really was. Hastily Cromwell gathered together a fleet under Admiral William Penn, and an army of some 2500 men under the command of General Robert Venables. He also appointed a council of three commissioners – Edward Winslow, Captain Gregory Butler, and Daniel Searle the governor of Barbados – to accompany the expedition.

At the last moment Cromwell summoned Spain's ambassador and told him bluntly that friendship between England and that country could exist on two conditions only – freedom of trade with the West Indies and complete religious liberty for Englishmen living in Spanish territories. The conditions, the ambassador replied, were impossible to grant: to demand them, he said, was like asking the King of Spain for his two eyes! Cromwell had probably expected this answer; it only decided him definitely in favour of the Western Design.

The expedition which he had gathered together, however, was perhaps the worst equipped and organised that ever left England. Although there were some good soldiers among the troops, the majority were, in the words of one of their number, 'common Cheats, Theeves, Cutpurses, and such like lewd persons'; in short, 'a wicked army' as the general's wife (who accompanied the expedition) described it, undisciplined, badly armed and poorly supplied. Besides, the secrecy with which the date of departure and destination of the expedition were surrounded, as well as the division of command between admiral, general and commissioners, was bound to cause suspicion and discord from the start.

The attack on Santo Domingo

Sailing from Portsmouth at the end of December 1654, the expedition made its first stop at Barbados five weeks later. Here, eleven Dutch ships then in the harbour were seized by Admiral Penn mainly for use as transports; food and arms were demanded and some 4000 men recruited for the army. These new recruits were later described by the General as 'so loose as not to be kept under discipline, and so cowardly as not to be made to fight'. In the Leeward Islands more recruits, of a slightly better type, were signed on, and from there the fleet set sail for Hispaniola where, according to the instructions, the troops were to make an overland attack on the capital city Santo Domingo.

A serious mistake was made by landing the men 50 kilometres from the city without sufficient supplies of food or water. Worn out by the long march and by sickness caused from drinking polluted water, mutinous and unruly the ragged army was thrown into panic and disorder by the first organised attack from Spanish lancers assisted by bands of local cattle hunters. Later an adjutant-general who had his sword broken over his head for his cowardly conduct during the fighting, declared that if everyone who had behaved the way he did had been similarly dealt with, there would not have been many whole swords left in the army! On the other hand there were some outstanding acts of courage, like that of Major General Haynes who on one occasion took on no less than eight Spaniards single-handed, killing one and wounding the rest. At the height of the battle, shortly before his death, he cried out that if only six brave fellows would stand by him he would soon force the enemy to retreat; but no one answered his call and he was killed soon after by a lance thrust. The complete massacre of the troops was averted only by the landing of a party of sailors to cover their flight back to the ship. As it was, a third of their number were dead or missing.

The capture of Jamaica

Fearful of Cromwell's anger at the failure at Santo Domingo, it was decided to attack some other Spanish island. Jamaica (which was known to be thinly populated and weakly defended) was the one chosen. On 10 May the fleet of thirty-eight ships with about 8000 men sailed into Kingston Harbour and anchored off Passage Fort. To prevent a repetition of the cowardice recently shown, it was ordered that whoever turned his back on the enemy was to be shot instantly by the soldier nearest to him. But the order was hardly necessary. There were no more than 1500 Spaniards in the island, of whom only some 500 could bear arms. A few shots fired into the little fort dispersed the defenders and soon the English flag waved above the walls of the fortification. The commanders of the expedition may have hoped to have been able to attack some stronger place from here later, but as it happened Jamaica was to prove the end of Cromwell's 'Design'.

The events of the next few days were confused. The Spaniards, who thought that the expedition's purpose was to plunder only, were astonished when handed the harsh surrender terms which included the provision that those of the inhabitants who wished to leave the island might do so. Venables gave the Spaniards time in which to consider these terms while he, unwisely, waited instead of following up his early success and marching on the capital.

The Governor, Juan Ramirez, was old and sick at the time. He was later deported by the English to Campeche in Central America, but died at sea. The handling of affairs fell largely to Christóval Arnaldo de Ysasi who, with Duarte de Acosta, eventually signed the peace terms. The Spaniards, meanwhile, had used the time given them to consider these terms to turn their cattle loose and escape with their valuables to the north coast and from there to Cuba, so that when the troops marched into Spanish Town they found it empty and bare of booty. In anger and disappointment they destroyed much of the town, burning the churches and melting the bells down for shot.

The Spaniards, however, did not give up their hope of recovering Jamaica. They had freed their slaves and left them behind in the mountains to harry the English with irregular warfare until it was possible to collect an army for the reconquest of the island. These freed slaves, later to become famous as the Maroons, were organised by Ysasi into an effective fighting force before he too escaped to Cuba. They were settled mainly in the hills of the St John district of St Catherine, still called Juan de Bolas after one of their chiefs (his real name was Juan Lubolo), on Vera-mahollis Savanna (Los Vermejales), and on the Rio Juana, the location of which is now uncertain.

Matters meanwhile were not going well with the English. Food had already become scarce, the situation being aggravated by the reckless slaughter – solely for the sake of the hides – of the wild cattle that roamed the surrounding plains. Supplies of clothing and medicine were also soon exhausted and disease and deadly fevers began to appear among the troops. At this juncture Penn, quickly followed by the suspicious Venables, decided to leave for England to report on conditions and explain away the failure at Santo Domingo. Cromwell had them both imprisoned in the Tower of London for their unsatisfactory conduct.

During this desperate and unsettled period the affairs of the island were administered as well as possible by successive military commissioners, four of whom died while doing their utmost to help the unfortunate infant colony. Efforts were made to suppress the Spanish ex-slaves, but they continued to be a menace, ambushing and killing many of the soldiers who ventured into the woods. The troops were constantly urged to plant food crops, but little or no cultivation was done, partly because of the activities of these freed slaves, but more because they believed that if there was no food they would be withdrawn and sent back to England. The result was famine and epidemics from which the men died like flies, crying with their last breath for bread! Ships from the fleet were sent out to attack Spanish shipping and raid the mainland ports. Prizes were taken and a certain amount of supplies captured, but not nearly enough to relieve the starvation that existed.

Cromwell was disappointed at the failure at Santo Domingo, but decided, nevertheless, to make the most of the new colony and to help it to the fullest. He issued his famous 'Proclamation giving Encouragement to such as shall transplant themselves to Jamaica'. It gave details of the grants of land which would be made to settlers, the rights they would enjoy in respect of fishing, the discovery of mines, quarries, et cetera. It also guaranteed them freedom from customs duties for a period of three years, and laid down that all persons born in the island should enjoy the same rights as the people of England. Supplies were sent out and a number of immigrants, including some Scotsmen of questionable character. Orders were issued for a thousand Irish girls and boys to be rounded up and transported to Jamaica, the former to become the wives of the soldiers, the latter servants of the officers, but it is doubtful that this order was ever carried out. White bondsmen[1] imported into the island did not stand up well to labour in Jamaica's hot climate and one of the Commissioners, Major General William Brayne, applied to Cromwell for an importation of African slaves, pointing out that as their masters would have to pay for them they would take more interest in their preservation and so work them with moderation.

Favourable accounts of the island attracted some 300 planters from New England; others came from Bermuda and Barbados. In December 1656, Luke Stokes, the elderly governor of Nevis, emigrated to Jamaica with his family and 1600 colonists, settling around Port Morant. The soil was fertile, but the area swampy and unhealthy. Within three months 1200 of the newcomers, including Stokes and his wife, had died! Today the names Stokesfield and Stokes Hall alone remain to remind us of these early settlers and their gallant old leader.

Brayne, last of the Commissioners, eventually died from fever, much to the grief of all for he seems to have ruled wisely and competently. Edward D'Oyley, a colonel in the army of invasion, was left in command of the colony. Twice before he had acted in this position, but, on each occasion, had been eventually replaced by Cromwell who was probably suspicious of him, knowing of his attachment to the monarchy. This time, however, D'Oyley was allowed to keep the command. He governed by court martial until June 1661 when, with the death of Cromwell and the restoration of

[1] See Chapter 10.

Charles II, king of England, Scotland and Ireland

Charles II to the English throne, he received his commission as the first civil governor of the island.

It was fortunate that the command fell at this time to as capable a military officer as D'Oyley, for he had barely taken over when the long-expected Spanish invasion came. Luckily, a dispatch from Bayona, the Governor of Cuba, to a Spanish sergeant-major giving detailed arrangements for the invasion fell into D'Oyley's hands. Sailing round the eastern end of the island rather than try to hack a way through the thick forests of the interior, D'Oyley and his force landed between the mouth of the White River and Ocho Rios. They successfully stormed a stockade which the Spaniards had built near Dunn's River, killing a number of the enemy and capturing their supplies.

But the Spaniards, especially their leader Ysasi, had not given up hope. A member of an old settler family, Ysasi, now officially appointed governor by the King of Spain, was determined to recapture the island. In May, 1658, another Spanish force, consisting mainly of contingents from Mexico, landed at Rio Nuevo. There, on a cliff near the river's west bank, they built a strong fort armed with cannon. As soon as news of the landing reached D'Oyley he called out 750 of his best officers and men and once more sailed round the island to the attack, arriving off Rio Nuevo on the morning of 25 June.

The English ships boldly entered the bay and, although under fire from the fort and opposed by two companies of Spaniards aided by some of their freed blacks, troops and supplies were landed and a camp set up. D'Oyley next dispatched his drummer with a letter to Ysasi calling on him to surrender in return for honourable terms and transport back to Cuba; but the latter sent him in reply a jar of sweetmeats and a courteous refusal. His position was strong, and he knew it; his troops outnumbered those of the English and the fort, perched as it was on top of a high hill with a river at the bottom, would be difficult to invade. But D'Oyley was equal to the challenge. By brave tactics and hard fighting the fort was stormed and the defenders routed. More than 300 Spaniards were killed and valuable supplies of food and arms captured, together with the Spanish royal standard and ten colours.

This battle, which took place on 27 June, made amends for the failure at Santo Domingo. It was the most important ever fought in Jamaica and put an end to Spanish hopes of reconquest, although the war was to drag on for two more years. It was now clear that without sea power the island could not be retaken, but the relieving fleet from Spain was unable to sail for the Caribbean because of Admiral Blake's naval victories and his tight blockade of the Spanish coast. Ysasi, who had escaped after the Rio Nuevo defeat, continued to hold out for two years in the mountains, hoping always for the relief which never arrived.

The final blow fell when Juan de Bolas and his party went over to the English side. With de Bolas's knowledge of the mountain trails and Spanish camp sites resistance now became impossible, and in 1660 Ysasi and the remnants of his followers escaped to Cuba in canoes. Ysasi was a brave and faithful servant of his king. In spite of great difficulties, he had fought hard for five years in defence of his country. With his departure all Spanish influence in Jamaica ended and the island was officially ceded to England by the Treaty of Madrid in 1670.

The defeat of the Spaniards removed the threat of foreign invasion, but in August of that same year D'Oyley found himself faced with a serious rebellion. It was led by two colonels, Raymond and Tyson, the latter having at the time the command of one of the regiments at Guanaboa Vale.

The reasons for the mutiny are not clear. Dislike of D'Oyley and his harsh methods no doubt played a part, as well as rivalry between those who favoured the Monarchy and those who preferred the Commonwealth; but the root of the matter probably lay in the fact that the men were tired of military rule and wished to settle down as colonists. They were no doubt encouraged by the fact that provisions were now plentiful, trade increasing and the general health of the people better.

D'Oyley, as usual, acted promptly to meet this new danger. Reinforcements were speedily brought up and the rebellious troops eventually persuaded to hand over their two leaders and to disperse peacefully in exchange for a complete pardon. Raymond and Tyson were tried by court martial and under a big tamarind tree in Mulberry Garden (where the Spanish Town Poor House now stands) were shot as traitors. Twelve days later the news of the Restoration of the Monarchy in England arrived and within a year D'Oyley received his commission as the first civil governor of Jamaica.

The instructions which accompanied the commission conferred to some extent the very privileges for which Raymond and Tyson had lost their lives, since among other things, D'Oyley was ordered to release the army and encourage planters, merchants and traders. Measures for the suppression of drunkenness and the encouragement of the Protestant religion were also thoughtfully included, as well as orders to set up courts of justice and to govern with the advice of a council of twelve persons.

D'Oyley, however, was a far better soldier than a civil administrator. Strong and capable, unaffected by the climate, he had taken over command at a most difficult time. He proved equal to the task and by his courage and ability had saved Jamaica at the battle of Rio Nuevo. But he did not take kindly to the new form of government and it was not long before he was replaced. He left the island in September, 1662, and died thirteen years later. Unfortunately we do not know what he was like in appearance: although his will mentions a picture and a vellum map of Jamaica, neither can be found today.

D'Oyley's successor, the handsome young Lord Windsor, was equally unsuited for the position (although for other reasons) and gave it up after little more than ten weeks! All the same, his short administration was important, if for no other reason than because his instructions formed the basis of the island's subsequent government. The most important clause in these instructions was that which gave the governor power, with the advice of the council, to call assemblies, although any laws passed were not to be in force for longer than two years, unless approved by the King.

Of importance also was the proclamation of Charles II, dated 14 December 1661, which the new governor brought with him. It stated, among other things, that the children of natural-born subjects of England,

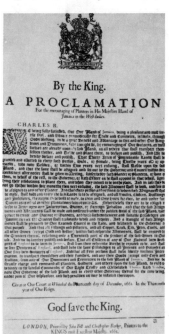

Charles II's Proclamation of 14 December 1661, encouraging English settlement of Jamaica

to be born in Jamaica, would be free citizens of England having the same privileges as English subjects. Windsor also brought out with him a mace and a seal for the island. The mace at present used in the House of Assembly is a later one. The original, which was thought to have been lost in the great earthquake that destroyed Port Royal in 1692, was only damaged at the time. There is evidence of its having been repaired shortly after, but no record of what later became of it. The seal bore the coat of arms that the King had granted to the island. It was designed by the Archbishop of Canterbury.

Windsor made general grants of land to the settlers, by which certain people benefited far more than others. Sir Thomas Lynch, Major Hope, Colonel Archbould and Sir William Beeston received the lion's share, the last three dividing about half the parish of St Andrew between them! If this method of making large land grants to a favoured few caused discontent, the expedition which Windsor launched against Santiago de Cuba earned him great popularity.

The war with Spain that had started as a result of Cromwell's Western Design ended formally with the Restoration of Charles II. In the West Indies, however, fighting never really ceased, and official encouragement was given to the buccaneers – a tough, wild collection of sea-rovers – to continue hostilities against the Spanish. By the time of the Restoration there was a considerable number of buccaneers at Port Royal and Captain Christopher Myngs, whom Windsor commissioned for the attack on Santiago, had no difficulty in mustering twelve ships and a thousand men for the purpose. Although strongly guarded by forts commanding the harbour, the town was captured with little difficulty and thoroughly sacked. In addition to a fortune in valuables, seven ships, a thousand barrels of gunpowder and thirty-four cannon (four of which were sent to the Tower of London) were captured.

Windsor, on the plea of 'being verie sick and uneesie', waited only long enough to secure his share of the plunder before sailing for England, leaving Sir Charles Lyttleton who had accompanied him to Jamaica, to act as Deputy Governor.

Chapter 5

The buccaneers

A feature of the first importance in Caribbean, as well as Jamaican history of this period, was the part played by the *buccaneers*, operating mainly from their base at Port Royal. The original buccaneers were the 'cow-killers' who had settled on the otherwise uninhabited north and west parts of Hispaniola. They were men of almost every nation, but mainly French, English and Dutch – runaway bondsmen, castaways, escaped criminals, political and religious refugees – who had sunk all other national rivalries in their sworn opposition to the Spanish. In the forests of Hispaniola roamed herds of wild cattle and pigs, descendants of the domestic animals of the early settlers. At first the activities of these men were limited to the slaughtering of these beasts to provide meat, hides and tallow which, in exchange for ammunition and rough stores, they supplied to the ships that occasionally put in at ports along the coast. They hunted with the help of dogs and for weapons used knives and long-barrelled muskets known as 'buccaneering-pieces'. They usually worked in pairs, each man having a partner with whom everything was shared.

The name 'buccaneer' comes from the French word *boucan* (adapted from a Carib term) referring to the frame used by the cow-killers for curing their meat, the method being to lay the meat, cut in long strips, on a hurdle of green wood to dry over a slow fire. Later when the buccaneers took to the sea they became known also as *filibusters* and *freebooters* – although many deserved the name of *pirate*. It was not until England and France began to commission these sea-rovers by granting them letters of marque, that is authority to act against a hostile nation, that their activities became technically legal and their status that of *privateers*.

Although these hunters harmed no one the Spaniards objected to their living in Hispaniola and tried to round them up with the help of lancers, without much success. An attempt to starve them into surrender by killing off or driving away the beasts they hunted had more effect, but the Spaniards were to pay dearly for their victory. Driven from their peaceful occupation and filled with hatred of their persecutors, the buccaneers turned pirates and got their own back by plundering Spanish property and killing every Spaniard they could.

Around 1630 the buccaneers moved from Hispaniola to the small neighbouring island of Tortuga. The Spaniards soon chased them out, but they were back the moment the coast was clear. Realising that their only hope of survival lay in unity, the buccaneers banded together into the 'Confederacy of the Brethren of the Coast'. At first they used only light craft, mainly canoes, but captured Spanish ships taken by surprise attack soon swelled their fleet, while with captured guns and arms they fortified Tortuga. Early successes brought them a flock of recruits and the stronger and bolder they grew the farther they raided.

Although lawless by calling, the buccaneers had a stern code of discipline which welded them into a dreaded fighting force. They usually sailed under carefully drawn-up articles, the first of which was, 'No prey, no pay'. All plunder went into one collection and was then divided according to the share-out scales and disability pensions as stated in the articles. The loss of a right arm, for instance, brought a compensation of 600 pieces-of-eight or 6 slaves; loss of a finger, 1 slave or 100 pieces-of-eight.

Much has been written about the cruelties of the buccaneers. It is told of the Frenchman, Francis L'Ollonais, for example, that he tortured prisoners to force them to tell where they had hidden their money and valuables, and tore out their tongues if they refused; that on one occasion he cut open the breast of a Spaniard with his cutlass and, tearing out the victim's heart bit and gnawed it! Roche Brasiliano, another buccaneer captain, is said to have roasted several Spaniards alive upon wooden spits, simply because they would not show him where they had their hog-yards.

Even if these stories are true – and there is reason to believe that they were exaggerated – the acts of the buccaneers can only be fairly judged in relation to the life of the times. They lived in an age of great brutality; many of them, like L'Ollonais, had worked as bondsmen (*indentured servants* they were called, but they were little better than slaves[1]) on West Indian plantations where they learnt lessons of cruelty by suffering it.

In Port Royal the buccaneers soon found what they needed most: a ready market for their Spanish loot, facilities for the repair and equipping of their vessels, and all the opportunities for amusing themselves the way they liked. And so they flocked to the port in ever growing numbers. At first they were welcomed and officially encouraged. But shortly after his accession to the throne, Charles II, although retaining Jamaica, tried by agreement to secure a trade with the Spanish Indies, and so decided to place a check on the buccaneers.

Sir Thomas Modyford

Early in 1664, Sir Thomas Modyford, a wealthy Barbadian planter, was appointed governor of Jamaica with strict instructions to suppress the buccaneers. He brought about a thousand settlers from Barbados with him. His measures against the buccaneers were not very successful. Driven from Port Royal, the Brethren went instead to Tortuga with their Spanish

[1] See Chapter 10.

prizes and booty. By November a drastic change of policy was recommended to Sir Thomas. The Second Dutch War had broken out and the Admiralty could not spare a fleet for the West Indies. The defence of the islands had to be based on the buccaneers and Modyford set to work to organise them into a regular striking force. As Long the historian was later to write, 'It is to the Bucaniers that we owe the possession of Jamaica at this hour'.

The French had been the first to try using the buccaneers as an organised fighting force, but without marked success. Modyford's attempt was to prove no better. He gathered a force of ten ships and 500 men and dispatched it under Colonel Edward Morgan (whose nephew Henry was to become the most famous buccaneer of all) to attack the Dutch islands of St Eustatius and Saba, whence, if successful, they should go on to Curaçao and the French-held island of Tortuga. But the project was too ambitious a one for so undisciplined a company. The buccaneers sailed on the usual 'no prey, no pay' condition and so looked for personal profit before serving any other cause. St Eustatius and Saba were captured easily enough, but quarrels over loot caused the rest of the project to fall through.

If the buccaneers were not very useful against the Dutch their merciless attacks on Spanish possessions were of great value since they kept the Spaniards occupied defending their own coasts and possessions. Modyford knew very well how important these activities were and encouraged them by arming the buccaneers with official commissions. In Henry Morgan he was to find his strongest ally, the tough, resourceful buccaneer leader who could hold the wild brethren together and direct their main efforts towards the defence of the island.

Henry Morgan

There is some uncertainty about Morgan's origin. Born about 1635, son of a Welsh land-owning farmer, he went to Barbados possibly as an indentured servant, making his way from there to Tortuga where he joined the buccaneers. He became a member of Mansvelt's crew and later, on the older man's death in 1667, its leader. Modyford, as we have seen, had employed Mansvelt, granting him letters of marque against Spain, this being (as he explained to his superiors in England) the only way of keeping the buccaneers from becoming the enemies of Jamaica. He was prepared to use Henry Morgan in the same way.

Morgan's first important exploit had the approval of the Council of Jamaica who authorised the Governor to commission him 'to take prisoners of the Spanish nation' in order to discover if there was truth in the rumour that the Spaniards intended to attack the island. Although Havana the capital of Cuba would have been the likeliest place at which to get the desired information, a council of war voted against an attack on this strongly fortified city. Instead, Morgan led his force of English and French buccaneers against Puerto Príncipe (now Camagüey), the second richest city in the island, 80 kilometres from the coast. The inhabitants who had been

Sir Henry Morgan, Welsh buccaneer

warned of the approaching force, moved out their valuables and prepared to resist the attack, surrendering only after a bloody house-to-house battle. Under torture the richer people disclosed the hiding places of their treasure and some were said to have confirmed the truth of the plan to attack Jamaica. Morgan was satisfied with the results, but not his men: the plunder when shared was so small that it was not sufficient to pay their debts in Jamaica. This probably suited the Welshman; as long as his men were hungry for gold he could entice them back to work, and for his next project – a raid on Porto Bello – they would need strong enticement.

Situated at the Caribbean end of the trade route across the Isthmus of Panama, Porto Bello was the third strongest city in America; it was also one of the wealthiest and Morgan stressed this fact, promising his followers rich gain as the prize for success. The French members of his crew refused to take part in the raid, but this did not discourage Morgan. Appealing to the bravery and greed of his remaining followers in a stirring speech, he pointed out that although their number was small their hearts were great, and anyway the fewer there were to share the spoil the more each man would get. His confidence was rewarded. With masterful, if brutal, tactics and brave fighting he captured the city. A relieving force sent from Panama was ambushed by the buccaneers and cut to pieces. While Morgan was at Porto Bello the Governor of Panama sent a sarcastic message to him, asking for a sample of the arms with which he had taken so great a city. Morgan gave the messenger a pistol and a handful of shot to take back to the Governor, with the promise that he would fetch them away himself, within a twelvemonth. He was not long in keeping his promise.

The buccaneers sailed from Porto Bello possibly to their favourite meeting place, a small rocky cay off the south-western end of Hispaniola called *Ile* (or *Isle*)-*à-Vache*, Cow Island, a name which the English corrupted to Isle of Ash. Here the vast loot of gold and silver, jewels, silks and other valuables, as well as some 300 black slaves, was divided according to the rules, the King and Modyford getting their share and Morgan his five per cent.

Back in Jamaica Morgan wrote his brief official report of the raid, leaving out most of the unpleasant details but making much of the fact that he had released eleven Englishmen from Porto Bello dungeons. Modyford was a little alarmed by the raid, for Morgan's commission empowered him to attack ships only, but there was not much he could do besides express his disapproval. The buccaneers were bringing great wealth into the country, and by attacking Spanish cities they kept the enemy forces occupied and so relieved the threat to Jamaica.

Soon Morgan and his men were on the move again, their destination Maracaibo, an important seaport in Venezuela, on the west shore of the strait joining the lake and gulf. Although again deserted by many of his captains, Morgan forced a way through the strait and plundered the town where, and later in Gibraltar at the head of the lake, he and his men spent weeks in making merry and drinking, and torturing the Spaniards to make them hand over their money and jewels. Once more by courage and crafty strategy, including the use of fire ships with which he dispersed a fleet he found blocking the retreat, Morgan and his small force triumphed over much larger numbers to return to their base at Port Royal with loot said to have amounted to a quarter million pieces-of-eight!

The buccaneers were joyously greeted by all – except the Governor. Dispatches had begun to arrive from London expressing the King's displeasure over the raid on Porto Bello, and holding Modyford answerable for it. Morgan was again reprimanded and his commission temporarily withdrawn; he was also advised to leave Port Royal for a time. This was a harsh blow for the buccaneer because he loved the gay and noisy life of the wicked port. It is said that one of his more pleasant fancies was to drag a winecask out into the street and, pistol in hand, threaten to shoot any passer-by who did not stop and drink with him! All the same, he understood the reasons for Modyford's action and so retired for a time to his country property and the company of Mary Elizabeth, his wife. Among his holdings were Dankes and Morgan's Valley in Clarendon, Llanrhumney in St Mary and Lawrencefield near Port Henderson where it is believed he died.

Soon Modyford could write to his superiors in London that all was peace and quiet, that most of the buccaneers, like Morgan himself, had become planters or merchants. But it was an uneasy peace, broken in the early part of 1670 by Spanish attacks on English shipping and a raid on the Jamaican coast by a man-of-war, in which plantations were burnt and the owners and their slaves carried off. Once more invasion rumours began to circulate and tempers to grow hot, especially when a boastful Spanish captain named

Pardal landed near Negril and nailed a statement to a tree claiming that he had raided English territory, and challenging Morgan to 'come out upon the coast and seek me, that he might see the valour of the Spaniards.' Two months later one of Morgan's captains, Morris, driven by strong winds into a bay off the east of Cuba, met and killed the boastful Pardal.

On 29 June the Council met in Spanish Town to consider what action should be taken. It was decided to commission Morgan once again, but now as 'Admiral and Commander-in-Chief of all the ships of war belonging to this harbour', with instructions, not only to destroy Spanish vessels, but also 'to land in the enemy's country as many of his men as he shall judge needful . . . and finally do all manner of exploits which may tend to the preservation and quiet of this island, being his Majesty's chief interest in the Indies'. This was exactly what Morgan wished: it opened the way for an attack on Panama City, something he had been planning for some time – his greatest and most daring exploit, and his last.

The attack on Panama City

Assembling his fleet of thirty-six ships in Bluefields Bay, Morgan sailed for Ile-à-Vache, from which in December, announcing that the taking of Panama stood most for the good and safety of Jamaica, he set sail. The island of Old Providence was captured on the way and used as an advance base for the attack on the strongly fortified town of Chagres on the Caribbean side of the Isthmus. The path to Panama was now open and Morgan with some 1200 men began his march on the city.

For more than eight days they were to stumble forward, hacking a way through the thick jungle, scorched by the blazing sun at times, then drenched by sudden tropical showers of rain; tormented by flies, mosquitoes and other stinging insects; harassed by stealthy Indians who shot their flights of arrows and vanished before a pistol could be cocked. The buccaneers had reckoned to live off the country and so carried almost no provisions, but the Spaniards, warned of their coming, had stripped the land as bare as possible of everything that could be eaten. To the other hardships, then, was added that of hunger, which as the days went by became so great that at one stage the buccaneers were forced to eat leather bags for food. Only Morgan's iron will and matchless leadership held the bearded, ragged, hunger-maddened men together and drove them steadily towards their glittering goal which they first glimpsed with joy on the evening of the ninth day.

Unlike the English who came to the Caribbean primarily to trade, the Spanish came to settle and build cities, amongst which Panama stood supreme. Besides the royal houses – including the Governor's palace, law courts and the treasury filled with gold and silver from Peru – there were 2000 merchants' homes and 5000 more belonging to tradesmen and people of lesser degree, as well as numerous chapels, monasteries, convents and other religious buildings, all with many fine towers; so high in fact was the tower of the cathedral, the Indians believed that the angels reached out from heaven to ring the bells.

In the plains before the city the buccaneers were met by a force of Spanish horse and foot soldiers led by the Governor, which outnumbered them three to one. But neither these, nor the wild bulls stampeded into the invaders' lines, nor the prayers of the people could save Panama. Steadily the tattered, faded flags of the rabble army advanced across the plains. A furious pitched battle was joined, soon ended by Morgan's masterful outflanking of the enemy. The Spanish survivors fled back to the city, but in a few hours all resistance was crushed.

Victory was followed by a scene of looting, torturing and wild celebration surpassing all others in the bloodstained history of the buccaneers. At the height of the revels a fire started, caused possibly by the blowing up of the powder magazines at the Governor's orders, which was to reduce the place to ashes. 'Thus', reported Morgan, 'was consumed the famous and ancient city of Panama.'

In February 1671, the buccaneers started on the return journey with 175 pack animals, mostly mules, laden with loot – gold and silver, jewellery and precious stones, treasure from the churches, rich vestments, plate, ornaments and other costly stuff – as well as 600 captives, men, women, children and black slaves. Most of the prisoners were sold and the rest ransomed later, bringing the total value of the Panama loot to 750 000 pieces-of-eight! But, after all the usual deductions were made, each buccaneer received only 200 pieces-of-eight. Some writers claim that Morgan cheated his men, but others deny he did. We will probably never know the full answer.

An uproarious reception greeted Morgan's return to Port Royal, including a formal vote of thanks from the Council of the island for the manner in which he had carried out his commission. But this time the Buccaneer and the Governor had gone too far. In July 1670 the Treaty of Madrid had been signed sealing peace between Spain and England and acknowledging the latter's right to hold American colonies, including Jamaica. Modyford did not know of this until Morgan had sailed from Bluefields. It is possible that he could have recalled the buccaneer before the landing on the Isthmus. Perhaps he tried. On the other hand both men may have decided to deliver the final blow to Spain's might in the Caribbean, whatever the consequences . . . and these were to follow swiftly after the news of Panama reached Europe.

Spain's ambassador protested strongly and demanded satisfaction. Some action had to be taken. Accordingly, in June 1671, Sir Thomas Lynch came out to replace Modyford as governor and to send him a prisoner to England where, on arrival, he was shut up in the Tower of London. Morgan followed in April of the following year, to answer for his part in breaking the Treaty of Madrid. But the recall of both men was only meant to soothe Spain's anger; Sir Thomas lived in ease and comfort while in prison and the buccaneer was entertained as a hero in London, spending riotous nights in the company of gay young nobles, including the Duke of Albemarle who was later to be appointed governor of Jamaica.

Eventually the two daring and far-sighted friends were cleared of all disgrace and, by a surprising change in policy, Morgan was knighted and made Lieutenant-Governor of the island, King Charles expressing 'particular confidence in his loyalty, prudence, and courage, and long experience of that colony'. In which office, as well as Custos of Port Royal and Judge of the High Court of Vice-Admiralty, Sir Henry was to serve efficiently. Modyford was rewarded with the post of Chief Justice and so were the two friends reunited. On his tombstone in the Cathedral, Spanish Town, Modyford is described as 'The Soule and Life of all Jamaica, Who first made it what it now is'.

The end of buccaneering

But the heyday of buccaneering was fast drawing to a close. To the big property owners and merchants it had brought wealth, but to the small proprietors disaster. The great planters could replace the white indentured servants who ran away and joined the Brethren by black slaves, but the small proprietor could not. Jamaica began to be a land of large estates run by slave labour. In time even the big planters came to mistrust the benefits of buccaneering. The stage was now being set for the new policy of attracting the trade of the Spanish Indies into English hands with Jamaica as one of the principal centres, so the interference of the buccaneers became undesirable. The fact is that by removing the Spanish threat to Jamaica so effectively the old sea-rovers had worked themselves out of a job, but many failed to understand this and ended with a rope around their necks at Gallows Point on the Palisadoes (often on Morgan's orders) because they would not give up their old way of life. Sir Thomas Lynch, governor from 1671 to 1675, was active in suppressing the Brethren, and although his successors Lord Vaughan and the Earl of Carlisle (with Morgan as Lieutenant-Governor) and later the Duke of Albemarle were less strict, the day of the Jamaica buccaneer was at an end.

Albemarle's private physician, Sir Hans Sloane,[1] attended Morgan shortly before the latter died. At the age of 53 the retired buccaneer was sick and old beyond his years, 'much given to drinking and sitting up late'. Sloane found him lean, sallow-coloured, his stomach jutting out. He, and a black medicine man to whom Morgan sometimes resorted, did their best for their patient, but on 25 August 1688, he died, probably from tuberculosis, and was buried on the Palisadoes as the guns of Fort Charles and those of all the ships in the harbour fired a last salute.

Like Morgan, Port Royal's end was drawing near. From a mere

[1] Man of letters, naturalist, collector, Sloane was also a physician of international fame who became known to history as 'the Jamaica doctor'. In the fifteen months spent in Jamaica as private physician to the Duke of Albemarle, he collected more than 800 new natural history specimens, as well as numerous drawings of the items he could not preserve, and these, together with his voluminous notes, formed the basis of his Latin *Catalogue of Jamaica Plants*, published in 1696, and of his *Voyage to the Islands Madera, Barbados, Nevis, S. Christopher's and Jamaica* dealing with Jamaica's natural history, published in two volumes, the first in 1707 the second 18 years later. He left his priceless collections to the nation, becoming as a result the founder of the British Museum. He died in 1753 at the age of 93.

careening place (*Cayo de Carena*, as the Spaniards called it) where ships might be beached and their hulls scraped clean of barnacles, the settlement, christened Port Royal in honour of the Restoration, rapidly became the island's most important seventeenth-century town. Stronghold of the buccaneers, trading centre of the island, chief market and clearing house for the slave trade, the town earned the reputation of being the richest and wickedest.

With a population of some 8000 people, its vast warehouses and cut-stone homes as dear-rented as if they stood in the streets of London, the Port was at the very height of its fame when on 7 June 1692, came destruction in the form of a violent earthquake which plunged half the town into the sea, together with the burial ground and Morgan's grave. More than 2000 people lost their lives, but there was one notable survivor, the Frenchman Lewis Galdy. Swallowed by one earthquake shock, he was by another spewed forth again alive into the sea from which he was rescued to live for many years longer. His tombstone with the story of his deliverance may be seen in the churchyard of Port Royal's parish church.

The government decided to abandon the stricken town and found a new settlement across the harbour, soon to be known as Kingston. But in spite of the earthquake and later disastrous fires and hurricanes, Port Royal survived to become an important naval station in the following century.

A contemporary print showing the destruction caused by the Port Royal earthquake of 7 June, 1692

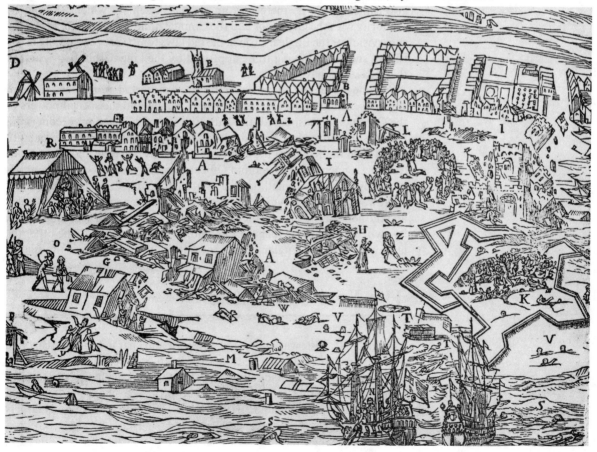

Chapter 6

The two invasions

The young colony was to weather two early invasions: the first, of its constitutional rights, in 1678;[1] the second, of its shores by a foreign enemy, sixteen years later. As we have seen, with the final defeat of the Spanish defenders of the island, military rule was brought to an end and civil government established. Under Lord Windsor, who followed D'Oyley as governor, a start was made with what is known as representative government; that is, there was an elected Assembly which, sharing its authority with the Governor and the Council nominated by him, under the supervision of the English Crown, passed laws for the proper running of the island, such laws having to be approved by the king within two years, or they ceased to have force.

As time passed the young Assembly grew more and more aggressive and vigorous, disregarding the rights of the Council and the special powers of the Crown and grasping all the authority it could. These proceedings did not pass unnoticed in England, although no strong action was taken until 1677. Then the King, on the advice of the Lords of Trade and Plantations (the forerunners of the Colonial Office), decided to check the Assembly's power by changing its method of legislation to that in force in Ireland under what was known as Poyning's Law. The difference between the old system and the new was that in one the island made its own laws in accordance with its own needs and sent them to England for approval, and in the other the laws were made in England and sent out for the approval of the island.

The Earl of Carlisle

The Earl of Carlisle was appointed governor and charged with the carrying out of this change. He arrived on 19 July 1678 with, for the Assembly's approval, forty ready-made laws framed by the King, including one to grant a perpetual revenue to the crown. The proposed change was respectfully but firmly opposed and all forty laws rejected by the Assembly largely

[1] See also Chapter 16.

50

on the ground that such a system of legislation was contrary to the government of England and placed too much power in the governor's hands.

A bitter struggle followed during which the Assembly was dissolved a number of times, the Governor on one occasion calling the troublesome members, 'fools, asses, beggars, cowards'! – but to no purpose for the Assembly remained fixed in its determination. Carlisle then turned on his chief opponents, Samuel Long[1] (Chief Justice and a member of the Council) and William (afterwards Sir William) Beeston (Speaker of the House). Both were eventually arrested and sent to England to answer to the Crown for leading the resistance by the Assembly. Long was summoned before the King in Council where he so ably defended the cause of the island that Carlisle's instructions were cancelled and the old method of legislation restored. This form of constitutional government for which those early Jamaican patriots fought so well, was to continue for nearly two centuries, until it was surrendered in 1866 for reasons that will be mentioned.

Du Casse's raid

The other invasion – the most serious attempt by a foreign power to capture the island in its entire history as a British colony – took place two years after the Port Royal earthquake. In 1689 war had broken out between England and France, the effects of which were early felt in the West Indies. Towards the end of 1692 a naval squadron commanded by Sir Francis Wheeler was sent from England to attack Martinique and the French settlements in Hispaniola. The attempt on Martinique failed and further operations were halted by heavy losses from disease which broke out among the troops. The presence of the fleet in the West Indies, however, kept the French on the defensive and prevented them from taking advantage of the disorganisation caused by the Port Royal earthquake and attacking the island. The Governor of French Hispaniola at the time was a well-known buccaneer named Jean du Casse who was determined to attack Jamaica as soon as Wheeler's ships left the West Indies. He did not have to wait long.

As soon as he could he let loose his filibusters on the island and they were able to carry out daily raids without meeting much resistance. But these were only preliminaries to the major attack which du Casse himself was planning. Fortunately a Captain Elliott who had been captured by the French and imprisoned in Petit Goâve on the west coast of Hispaniola, managed to escape to Jamaica in a small canoe in time to warn the Governor, Sir William Beeston, that du Casse was about to attack with a large force of over twenty ships and more than 3000 men, mostly

The second Earl of Carlisle

---

[1] Samuel Long came out to Jamaica at the age of seventeen with the army of occupation as secretary to the Commissioners. Stripped of all his offices by the Earl of Carlisle, he was reappointed Chief Justice by the Earl's successor Sir Thomas Lynch. He died here and is buried in the Cathedral, Spanish Town. His great grandson Edward Long (1734–1813) famous as the historian of Jamaica, was also Speaker of the House of Assembly and Judge of the Vice-Admiralty Court.

buccaneers. Elliott was later rewarded by King William III with the gift of a gold chain and medal as well as £500 in cash.

Realising that it was impossible to protect the whole coastline, Beeston decided to leave the eastern part of the island unguarded and to defend the most important coastal points. Martial law was proclaimed and every officer ordered to his post. Fort Charles, Port Royal, was repaired, a fortification built in the Kingston Parade, the narrow pass at Rock Fort guarded and breastworks thrown up at Old Harbour and Carlisle Bay in the old parish of Vere, or Withywood, originally so called, it is said, because of the thick forests and abundance of withes.

On 17 June 1694, du Casse's fleet of three warships and twenty-three transports came in sight with a fresh gale. Landings were made at Port Morant and Cow Bay, the former place later becoming the headquarters of the invasion. The forces marched inland, burning plantations and destroying over fifty sugar-works, kidnapping hundreds of slaves, murdering or torturing any white colonists who fell into their hands, and demanding terrible tribute in true buccaneer fashion. 'More inhuman barbarities were never committed by Turk or infidel', the governor was later to declare.

When they had completed their work of destruction in this part of the island, the forces returned to their ships and the fleet set sail. Moving westward along the coast du Casse deceived the defenders into thinking that he intended to attack Port Royal, but sailed instead to Carlisle Bay, clearly with the object of marching inland and capturing Spanish Town. But here he was met by militia companies of planters supported by their slaves, many of whom went straight into battle footsore and hungry from a hurried 58-kilometre march from Spanish Town. The defenders also made determined stands in property houses in the neighbourhood which the French failed to take, losing many officers and men in the attempts. Giving up hope of conquering the island, the invaders contented themselves with destroying the small town of Carlisle and doing whatever harm they could before withdrawing to their ships and returning to Petit Goâve.

Although the island had been saved, it had suffered very severely from the attack. In addition to about 100 killed or wounded, many plantations had been burnt, 50 sugar works destroyed, and about 1300 slaves as well as enormous loot carried off. It is said that the French lost 700 men in all. Counterattacks by English ships from Jamaica against French Hispaniola were not very successful; meanwhile the war dragged to a close, ending in September 1697 with the Treaty of Ryswick. By the treaty Spain recognised the French claim to the western part of Hispaniola which, as we have seen, had been settled by the buccaneers in the face of strong Spanish opposition. The French called their colony St Domingue and the Spanish called theirs Santo Domingo. Today the island is still shared, but now by the two independent states of Haiti and the Dominican Republic.

The War of the Spanish Succession

The peace which followed did not last long. On the death of King Charles II

*Vice-admiral John Benbow,
English naval officer*

of Spain in November 1700, Philip of Anjou, a grandson of King Louis XIV of France, succeeded to the Spanish throne. This combination of France and Spain became an immediate threat to the safety of the other European nations who began to form alliances to meet the danger. War was the result – the War of the Spanish Succession, as it is called – which started in 1702 when England and the Netherlands declared war on France and Spain. It was brought to an end eleven years later by the Treaty of Utrecht.

The main fighting took place in Europe, but in the West Indies where the safety of the various colonies depended on the naval strength of their respective mother countries, the coming and going of rival fleets was of the first importance. Shortly before the war started, Vice-Admiral John Benbow had arrived in the West Indies with a fleet which he based at Port Royal for the defence of Jamaica. The French met this danger by sending out a fleet of their own under the Count de Château-Renault which took up its position in Hispaniola. Château-Renault did not remain in these waters long, and on his departure Benbow sailed from Jamaica in search of a small squadron commanded by du Casse, which he encountered off Santa Marta, Colombia, on 19 August. The action fought is memorable chiefly because of Benbow's obstinate courage. With one leg shattered by chain shot, he continued to direct operations until the desertion of some of his captains forced him to give up chasing the enemy. On his return to Port Royal he court-martialled his officers, two of whom were sentenced to be shot. He himself died there of his wounds and was buried in the Kingston Parish Church where his tomb may still be seen.

Chapter 7

The early eighteenth century (1703–1728)

Under the Treaty of Utrecht, by which the war ended, Britain[1] was awarded the Contract, or *Asiento*, previously held by France, for supplying Spanish settlements in the New World with slaves. This was the most important provision of the peace as far as the British West Indies were concerned, with Jamaica benefiting most of all, for the island became the distribution centre for the trade, the majority of the slaves being shipped from here to Spanish ports in vessels locally owned and manned.

But all was not well with the island. Continuing its aggressive policy, the Assembly was constantly at loggerheads with the governors who represented the Crown, especially over money matters – the voting of funds to support the troops stationed here for the defence of the island, and the provision of a Perpetual Revenue referred to in the last chapter. As already mentioned, the form of constitution existing in Jamaica required that the laws passed be approved within two years by the King, which was done in return for the granting, by the Assembly, of a perpetual revenue to the Crown, chiefly for the running expenses of the government and the upkeep of the forts. Grudgingly the Assembly had passed two acts, each securing the revenue for twenty-one years, but now refused to pass a third. As a result the laws lay unapproved in England.

Eight governors followed one another during this period, some good administrators, other less good, all failing to control the troublesome Assembly. So bitter did the quarrels become that one night the House (which then met in Spanish Town) was entered and the Journals torn up and thrown into the street. In spite of a £500 reward the guilty persons were never discovered. Disorders reached the point of riot during Sir Thomas Handasyde's governorship when on 3 April 1710, in the course of a stormy session of the Assembly, some members drew their swords and threatened the Speaker of the House, young Peter Beckford. His cries for help brought his father, the Governor and guards to his rescue. The doors of the chamber

[1] In 1706 an Act of Union was passed declaring that England and Scotland (which had been united under one sovereign since 1603) should have a united Parliament as from 1 May 1707. From this time it is proper to speak of British rather than English activities in the West Indies.

were forced open and the Assembly dissolved in the Queen's name. The incident, however, caused the death of the elder Beckford who, it is said, slipped and fell down the stairs and died as a result. In another account we are told that he suffered a stroke while running with the Governor to the House of Assembly and collapsed in the Parade; he was later found by candlelight and put on a cot, but never revived. A former Lieutenant-Governor of the island, President of the Council and first Custos of Kingston, Beckford was one of the richest West Indian proprietors who ever lived. He owned twenty-two plantations and nearly four thousand slaves, and died leaving over £1 000 000 in personal property.

Meanwhile, in spite of the peace treaty of 1713, relations between Britain and Spain continued to be those of enemies. In the Caribbean, quarrels arose out of illicit slave trading by the British and the refusal of the Spanish to recognise the British colony that had been established at Belize or the trading stations on the Mosquito Coast. Spanish attacks on British ships led to similar action by the British. In 1718 war with Spain broke out. It came to an end three years later with the Treaty of Madrid.

The war had no direct effect on Jamaica, but the island had troubles enough of its own. Epidemics raged and violent hurricanes caused serious loss of life and property. The hurricane of 28 August 1722, left only six out of fifty ships afloat in Kingston Harbour and caused the water to rise 5 metres above the usual mark at Port Royal. Troubles with the Maroons added to the general confusion, as did attacks by pirates who were now plaguing the Caribbean in growing numbers. Coastal vessels were constantly molested by them and isolated plantations plundered. On one occasion Nicholas Brown, or the 'Grand Pirate' as he was known, together with his companion Christopher Winter, burnt down a house in St Ann near the coast with sixteen people locked in it! A reward of £500 for his capture was earned by John Drudge who had been to the same school at Port Royal as Brown when both were boys. Captured after a fight on one of the South Cays of Cuba, Brown died of his wounds on the way to Jamaica, but Drudge, not to be cheated of the reward, cut off the pirate's head, pickled it in a keg of rum and produced it in Jamaica in support of his claim!

A Proclamation of 1717 offering the King's Pardon to any pirate who surrendered within a stated time had some effect, a number giving themselves up in Jamaica and Bermuda. On the other hand many refused to abandon piracy, and even some who took advantage of the Pardon later slipped back into their old occupation.

'Blackbeard' and 'Calico Jack'

Among the pirates who flourished at this time was Edward Teach, or 'Blackbeard', believed to have been born in Jamaica, although some accounts state Bristol, and others Carolina. A powerful giant of a man, Teach is said to have struck terror into the hearts of his enemies by going into action often with flaming matches plaited into his flowing black beard. He was eventually killed in a sea fight off North Carolina.

Anne Bonney (above) and Mary Read were women pirates and two of 'Calico Jack's' toughest crew members

After a successful career of robbery and murder, Captain Charles Vane, another notorious pirate of this period, was captured, brought to Jamaica and hanged at Gallows Point. Perhaps the most romantic of the lot was Jack Rackham, or 'Calico Jack' as he was called because of his fondness for wearing calico underclothes, who started his career as a member of Vane's crew, rising in time to be leader. After terrorising the Caribbean for more than two years he made the mistake of lingering too long on Jamaica's north coast during November, 1720. News of his presence at Ocho Rios was carried to Sir Nicholas Lawes, governor at the time, who, determined to do his best to stamp out piracy, immediately sent Captain Barnet and a swift sloop in pursuit. Barnet found Rackham anchored in Negril Bay, enjoying a rum punch party, and after a short running fight captured him and his crew. At the trial in the Court of Vice-Admiralty, Spanish Town, it was discovered that two of Rackham's toughest crew members were really women disguised as men – Anne Bonney and Mary Read. Both were condemned to death, but Anne seems to have escaped punishment and Mary died of fever in prison at Port Royal before sentence could be carried out. 'Calico Jack' was executed and his body squeezed into an iron frame and hung up on a sandy islet off Port Royal (still called Rackham's Cay) as a warning to other pirates of the fate that awaited them in Jamaica.

The beginnings of prosperity

The administration of Sir Nicholas Lawes saw a number of interesting and important developments, including the setting up of the first printing press by Robert Baldwin in Kingston in 1717, a result of the encouragement that Lawes gave to printing and learning generally. An early and now very rare publication of Baldwin's was an account of 'The Tryals of Captain John Rackam, and other Pirates'. There are copies of this pamphlet in the Public Record Office, London.

An enterprising planter and property owner, Lawes it was who introduced coffee into the island from Hispaniola, planting it at his Temple Hall estate in 1728. He did his best to solve the problems which had caused so much bitterness and trouble in the Assembly and to pave the way for the passing of the Revenue Act. This, however, did not take place until 1729 when General Robert Hunter was governor. By it £8000 annually was paid to the Crown and in return all the laws passed in the island were approved by the King. For more than a century after this the constitutional rights of Jamaica were to remain undisturbed.

In spite of war conditions and serious internal difficulties, the early years of the eighteenth century saw the beginning of prosperity in Jamaica, as in the West Indies generally, and the rise in power and wealth of the island-born or *creole* proprietors. Politics and the country's economy were put on a sound footing; sugar production increased, while cattle breeding, log-wood and coffee cultivation proved more and more profitable. The same period saw also Kingston's rise in size and importance, the blossoming of theatre life, lavish entertainments and high living for the privileged rich.

Chapter 8

The Maroons

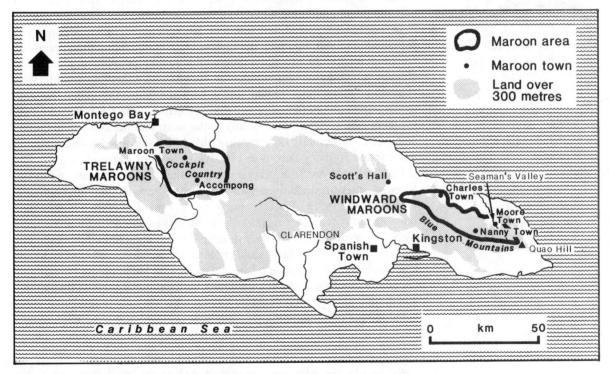

The Maroon areas of Jamaica

As shown in the last chapter, the wrangling and political problems that hindered the proper running of the government exposed the island to certain dangers, especially from the Maroons. The original Maroons, as we have seen, were the freed or runaway Spanish slaves who had retired to the thickly-wooded interior parts of the island. The name Maroon probably derived from the Spanish *cimarrón* meaning 'wild', 'untamed'. First employed by their previous masters to harass the English invaders, one band under a chief named Juan de Bolas later turned against the

Skilled in woodcraft, the Maroon warrior usually avoided an open fight, preferring to attack from ambush

Spaniards and helped in their final defeat. Those who went over to the English side were rewarded with grants of land, de Bolas was made colonel of a black regiment of militia and for a time trouble ceased. But all the Maroons had not been won over. Other bands continued to live free in the woods, hunting the wild pig and growing enough plantain, corn and yams for their own needs. The majority, in fact, disapproved of de Bolas's action and he was eventually ambushed and murdered by his own people.

Within a year of the arrival of the English in the island Major-General Robert Sedgewick, one of the Commissioners, predicted that the Maroons would become 'a thorn in the sides of the English'. His words were to prove truer than perhaps even he expected. As the island became more settled and plantations spread farther inland, the Maroons found it easier to swoop from the hills by night, set fire to the fields, and steal the cattle and stock. Runaway slaves from the new plantations swelled their number and gave them greater confidence. The offer made in 1663 of land and full freedom to every Maroon who surrendered was ignored, as we have seen, by all but de Bolas and his party. This failure to come to terms with the Maroons was to result in 76 years of irregular warfare, an expenditure of nearly £250 000 and the passing of some 44 Acts of the Assembly.

In time the original Maroons settled chiefly in the east and north parts of the island. In 1690, however, the slaves in Clarendon, consisting mainly of Coromantees[1] – an extremely brave and warlike people from the Gold Coast – rebelled and escaped into the woods where they soon established themselves. They later joined forces with the Maroons under the able leadership of one of their number named Cudjoe. With the help of his two brothers Accompong[2] and Johnny in the west, and the sub-chiefs Quao[3] and Cuffee in the east or windward side, Cudjoe started a campaign of murder and robbery known to history as the First Maroon War.

Concentrated on the northern slopes of the Blue Mountains and in the forested interior, including later the weird and almost impenetrable Cockpit Country, the Maroons developed a form of warfare which baffled most of the parties sent against them. Skilled in woodcraft and familiar with the untracked forests, they usually avoided open fight, but, disguised from head to foot with leaves and cunningly concealed, preferred to attack from ambush. The surprise of these attacks, plus the accurate shooting of the Maroons often brought them quick victory, but if pressed they rarely stood; instead, they took to the cover of the woods, only to reform at some suitable spot to prepare another ambush.

[1] Variously spelt Cromanty, Koromanti *et cetera*, this is in fact the name of a town and settlement area of the Gold Coast rather than of a tribe, but is used to cover broadly the Akan-speaking peoples. There are other such names (for example, Senegalese, Whydahs, Eboes, Mandingoes), generally used in contemporary accounts of West Indian plantation life which are similarly imprecise, and even misleading, as many refer only to the ports from which slaves were shipped.

[2] Accompong in St Elizabeth was called after him. The other permanent Maroon settlements which later came into existence were Trelawny Town (named for Edward Trelawny, governor from 1738–52), Scott's Hall, Charles Town and Moore Town.

[3] His name survives in Quao Hill in St Thomas-in-the-East.

It was almost impossible to surprise them in their settlements. Keen-eyed lookouts usually spotted an approaching force hours away and spread the warning, often by means of the *abeng*, a kind of bugle made from a cow's horn. Besides using it for sounding an alarm, the Maroons are said to have been able, by a particular call upon the horn, to summon each member of their party from afar 'as easily as he would have been spoken to by name, had he been near'.

British troops, unaccustomed to the country, the climate or method of warfare and worn out by long marches, suffered heavily in their clashes with the Maroons. Parties of seasoned settlers did little better. The building of a series of barracks and fortified posts with connecting roads as close as possible to the main Maroon settlements, as well as the use of dogs and Mosquito Coast Indians for tracking and fighting, had some effect at first. In 1734 Captain Stoddart led a successful attack on Nanny Town (named for a Maroon chieftainess, now a National Hero of Jamaica) high in the Blue Mountains. With the aid of small swivel guns, dragged up the steep mountain sides, the huts were blown to pieces and the villagers attacked as they ran in disorder, some even leaping off the cliffs to their death. The town was completely destroyed and never resettled. To this day it is believed to be haunted by the ghosts of those who died in that fight.

Finding his haunts less secure than they were, Cudjoe decided to move to the Cockpit area of Trelawny. Most of the Maroons who had escaped from Stoddart's attack moved farther inland to a new village site, and soon there was fighting again. Renewed efforts to suppress them, aided even by sailors, had varying success. On one occasion 200 seamen supported by the militia marched almost to the new village, but were forced back with heavy losses, by rain storms and Maroon attacks. There is a place in Portland still called Seaman's Valley which, it is believed, marks the spot where the sailors were defeated, but documents in the Jamaica Archives show that the name predates the event and is probably a personal name. Meanwhile, raids on plantations increased, as did the fear that the Maroon victories would encourage the slaves – now outnumbering the white colonists 14 to 1 – to rise in mass revolt.

By now the Assembly was sufficiently alarmed to vote the necessary funds for a large scale campaign against the Maroons. More Mosquito Indians as well as companies of free blacks and mulattoes were thrown into the fight. Pressed now on all sides and with most of their provision grounds destroyed, the Maroons found themselves in a desperate situation, faced with the alternative of surrender or starvation . . . but the government did not know this when, eager also for an end of the fighting, they commissioned a Colonel Guthrie in 1738 to seek out Cudjoe and offer him favourable terms of peace.

Suspicious at first of Guthrie's intentions, Cudjoe took all precautions against a surprise attack before showing himself. We are told that he was a short but extremely squat man, with a large lump of flesh upon his back and a strange wild manner. He was wearing that day a tattered old blue coat, white knee-pants, a head-tie and small round hat. He carried a long musket, powder horn, bag of shot and a machete in a leather sheath worn under the armpit.

After some discussion and the exchange of hats between Cudjoe and Guthrie as a sign of friendship, the treaty was agreed to on 1 March 1739 under a large cotton tree (known ever after as Cudjoe's Tree) growing in the centre of the cluster of Maroon huts at the entrance of the passage which led into Petty River Bottom Cockpit. By its terms the Maroons were guaranteed full freedom and liberty, were given 600 hectares of land lying between Trelawny Town and the Cockpits, and the right to hunt wild pigs anywhere except within a three-mile limit of towns and plantations. Cudjoe was appointed chief commander in Trelawny Town and his successors named in order beginning with Accompong and Johnny. The chief was empowered to inflict any punishment he might think proper for crimes committed by his people, except for those requiring the death sentence: such cases were to be handed over to a justice of the peace. Two white men, named by the governor, were to live permanently with the Maroons in order to maintain friendly contact between them and the colonists.

The Maroons, on their part, were to cease all hostilities, to receive no more runaway slaves but instead to help recapture them, a reward being paid for each so returned, and were required to assist the government in suppressing any local uprising or foreign invasion. The following year a similar treaty was made with Quao, chief of the Maroons left in the Blue Mountains – and the war was ended. More than fifty years of peace were to follow.

Chapter 9

War years

The period covered by this chapter (1739 to 1763) was one of almost continuous warfare, and it is in this setting that the events which took place in Jamaica must be viewed. The growing animosity between Spain and Britain came to a head in 1739 in the War of Jenkins's Ear. Again the chief cause of the war was the old one of illegal trading. Tension in the Caribbean grew with the stopping of British ships by Spanish *guarda costas* (patrol-vessels whose captains claimed the right of search) and the ill-treatment of the crews led to reprisals by the British.

In England, meanwhile, anger was being stirred up by stories of Spanish brutality to British sailors, especially the case of Mr Jenkins and his ear. A master mariner by profession, Robert Jenkins is said to have inherited a small fortune from his father in Jamaica and settled here. The story is told that he once drove off a party of Spaniards who were salvaging a Spanish wreck near the Florida coast and took the treasure from them as well as one of their ships. On a complaint being made by Spain, the Governor of Jamaica gave orders for Jenkins to be arrested, but he managed to escape. Unluckily for him he was later captured by a *guarda costa* and roughly handled by the captain who, he said, slashed off one of his ears and told him to take it to England as a warning of the fate awaiting British seamen who broke Spain's trade laws.

Some people who knew the kind of man Jenkins was felt that both his ears were still safely under his wig. Nevertheless, the story, true or false, had its effect, especially when Jenkins appeared before a committee of the House of Commons in England with a shrivelled, leathery object which he said was his ear! When asked what were his thoughts during his ill-treatment, he answered: 'I recommended my soul to God, and my cause to my country'. So great was the resulting clamour for vengeance that in spite of the opposition of the Prime Minister, Sir Robert Walpole, Britain declared war on Spain on 19 October 1739.

Once more the Caribbean began to stir with naval activity as the privateers and warships of both nations went into action. Admiral Edward Vernon[1] who had boasted in the House of Parliament that he could capture

[1] In an effort to reduce drunkenness among the crews, Vernon (nicknamed 'Old Grog' from his grogram coat) ordered the neat rum issued to men and officers to be diluted with water. To this day the mixture is known as *grog*.

Porto Bello with six warships only, was given the command of a squadron, with instructions to destroy the Spanish settlements in the West Indies and to distress their shipping. With six ships, as he had promised, he captured Porto Bello, took possession of all vessels in the harbour, carried off the brass guns and blew up the forts, returning triumphant to Port Royal, as England rejoiced wildly at the news.

'They now *ring* the bells, but they will soon *wring* their hands', Sir Robert Walpole said when war was declared on Spain. His words were soon to prove true, for with the Porto Bello campaign the spectacular victories ended: disaster lay ahead. Refitting his ships at Port Royal, Vernon sailed for Cartagena which he attacked without success, while Captain Knowles (later to become admiral and governor of Jamaica) captured the little town of Chagres which Henry Morgan had used seventy years before as the base for his attack on Panama City.

Meanwhile the rumour that France intended to support her ally Spain by sending a fleet to capture Jamaica, resulted in the arrival at Port Royal in January 1741, of Rear-Admiral Sir Chaloner Ogle and a powerful fleet with 12 000 troops. Once more it was decided to attack Cartagena, using this great force, increased now by nearly 4000 men from the North American Colonies, and a black Jamaican contingent. Again the venture failed. Bad leadership by Brigadier-General Robert Wentworth, the inexperienced commander of the troops, quarrels between himself and Admiral Vernon, and an appalling outbreak of yellow fever among the soldiers turned early success into a disastrous and costly failure. Back in Jamaica the fever-ridden men were encamped at Greenwich near Hunt's Bay. There, close to mosquito-breeding swamps, the epidemic raged with renewed fury and spread soon to Kingston taking hundreds of lives.

An attack on Santiago, Cuba, led again by Vernon and Wentworth, failed for the same reasons as that on Cartagena and cost the lives of more than a thousand soldiers. Not content, however, an even more ambitious plan was determined upon – an attack on Panama City. Fresh troops were sent from England, and Governor Trelawny, who had decided to accompany the expedition, raised a regiment in the island and placed himself at its head. He knew that the other military operations had failed largely because of the rivalry of the two commanders and he hoped he could keep the peace between them. But, as before, they quarrelled, while the deadly fever continued its work, over 900 men dying from it on the way. In the end the attack was abandoned and the force returned to Jamaica, Vernon and Wentworth being later recalled to England. Their useless campaigns had cost the lives of some 20 000 men!

France came into the fighting on Spain's side in 1744, and the war dragged on for four years more, ending with the Treaty of Aix-la-Chapelle. The peace brought no settlement of any important questions between France and England in the West Indies, and no reference was made in the treaty to one of the chief causes of the war, the Spanish claim to the right of searching British ships for contraband.

It was fortunate for Jamaica that she had at this time as competent a governor as Edward Trelawny. A firm but tactful man he had good relations with the Assembly, and his fourteen-year administration (the second longest in the island's history) was, apart from a violent hurricane in October 1744, and an unsuccessful slave conspiracy the following year, almost free from local troubles.

The hurricane, which was accompanied by an earthquake, almost destroyed Port Royal; the fortifications at Mosquito Point (later known as Fort Augusta) were badly damaged, all the wharves and warehouses in Kingston, Passage Fort and Old Harbour swept away, and only one out of 105 ships then in Kingston Harbour managed to ride out the storm. The slave conspiracy which had as its object the murdering of all white people in the island, would, had it developed, have had far-reaching effects. But the plot was betrayed by a black nanny because the conspirators refused to agree to her request that the life of the white child she was employed to nurse should be spared. About ten of the ringleaders were executed and others deported.

Admiral Knowles, who followed Trelawny as governor, is remembered chiefly for his attempt to transfer the capital from Spanish Town to Kingston in 1755. In so doing he lost the popularity he had enjoyed as the naval commander in Jamaica, and disturbed the harmony among the people which Trelawny had managed to build up. Opinion divided sharply over the question of the change of capital: it was favoured by the Kingston merchants and the people of the eastern parishes, and strongly objected to by the residents of Spanish Town and of the parishes to the west. In spite of bitter opposition, Knowles succeeded in getting the Act for the removal passed, by which various Public Offices as well as the island's official Archives were transferred to Kingston. Petitions to England eventually resulted in the disallowance of the Act, but by then more than three years had gone by and Knowles had resigned his governorship to rejoin the navy. Shortly after the new governor, Henry Moore, announced the disallowance of the Act, the island's Archives were loaded on to thirty wagons, and, with a strong military guard, carried back to Spanish Town amidst great rejoicing. Illuminations, firework displays and other entertainments marked the event, including the burning in the Parade of an effigy of Admiral Knowles.

Slave revolts

In 1760 the most serious slave revolt in the island's history broke out in St Mary, spreading later almost throughout the country. The references made so far to revolts and conspiracies will have shown that many of the slaves refused meekly to accept the bondage into which they had been thrown. In fact, they did not always wait until they had arrived in the West Indies to start their resistance: many slave-trading voyages ended in failure because of mutiny among the slaves. On the plantations precautions were taken to prevent the possibility of escape or revolt, but the slaves often found a way out. As early as 1678, while Sir Henry Morgan was acting as governor, there is mention of a serious slave revolt. Other uprisings took place during the seventeenth and early eighteenth centuries, including the conspiracy of 1745, and were vigorously suppressed; but that of 1760 was of a different order.

It is known as Tacky's Rebellion, after its leader, a Coromantee slave who had been a chief in Africa. Laying his plans with great care and in secrecy, he and a small party of trusted followers, mostly Coromantees like himself and mainly from Frontier and Trinity plantations, stole down to Port Maria before daybreak on Easter Monday, murdered the drowsy storekeeper of the fort and made off with a supply of muskets, powder and shot. By dawn hundreds of slaves had joined Tacky. They moved inland according to plan, overrunning the estates and killing the surprised or sleeping white settlers. At Ballard's Valley the rebels, happy at their victory, paused for a celebration.

Meanwhile a slave from Esher, one of the properties that had been overrun, had slipped away and spread the alarm. A troop of 70 to 80 mounted militia was soon mustered and on its way to the trouble area. Messages were also sent overland to the Governor in Spanish Town who promptly dispatched two companies of regular troops and called out the Scott's Hall Maroons who, as we have read, were obliged by their treaty with the government to assist in such an emergency.

The engagements that followed were fought with great skill and daring by the slaves. To their natural bravery was added the encouragement of the obeahmen who distributed a powder among Tacky's followers which, it was believed, would protect them from injury in battle. The obeahmen claimed that they themselves could not be killed. Learning of this, the troops made a determined effort and captured one of them. They hanged him at a prominent place, painted and dressed up as he was in his mask, ornaments of teeth and bone and feather trimmings.

With their faith in the power of obeah shaken, a number of the rebels lost heart and returned to their plantations, but Tacky and a small band continued the struggle until overcome by greater numbers. Fighting free, he and some twenty-five of his men took to the woods, chased by the Maroons. One of them, a sharpshooter named Davy, eventually caught up with Tacky and while both were running at full speed, he raised his musket and with the deadly aim for which he was noted, shot the rebel leader dead. The rest of Tacky's men were later found in a cave where they had killed themselves rather than be captured.

By this time slave revolts were breaking out in other parishes. An uprising of Coromantees in Westmoreland proved almost as serious as Tacky's rebellion. Again Maroons helped in suppressing it. Other conspiracies, a number of which were found out and quelled before trouble started, flared up in St Thomas-in-the-East, St John,[1] Kingston and St James. Months were to pass before peace returned to the island, but by then sixty white people and between three and four hundred black slaves had lost their lives, including those executed as ringleaders, two of whom were burnt alive and two others hung in iron cages on the Kingston Parade and left to starve to death.

---

[1] An old parish which was merged with that of St Catherine in 1867.

The Seven Years' War

Morro Castle, fortress built by the Spanish to protect the city and harbour of Havana

In spite of the Treaty of Aix-la-Chapelle there was little peace in the Caribbean and by 1756 Britain was at war with France, Spain coming in two years later on the French side. Besides the European campaigns, the war included those of Wolfe in Canada and Clive in India. In the West Indies nearly every French island fell to the British, and Havana, capital of Cuba, was invaded by an expeditionary force to which Jamaica contributed considerably. The combined sea and land forces sailed to the attack from Barbados in April 1762, being joined off St Domingue by the ships of the Jamaica naval station commanded by Commodore Sir James Douglas, together with a contingent of men from the island consisting of white officers, free coloured volunteers and black slaves.

By skilful tactics and hard fighting the great Morro Castle, guardian of the harbour and city, was captured and Havana surrendered to the British. Among the victorious troops was a slave called Cuffee for whom the invasion was to bring freedom.[1] Taken eight years before by ship from

[1] The story is recorded in the St Catherine *Vestry Minutes*, 1761–9, 15 June 1763, now in the Jamaica Archives.

Jamaica to the Bay of Honduras, he was later sold to a Don Emanuel who owned a plantation in the mountains of Cuba. On the landing of the British, Cuffee ran away from the plantation and was signed on as a volunteer in the 46th Regiment. Later, back in Jamaica, he was given his freedom for the part he played in the capture of Havana. Perhaps Cuffee's worst moment came shortly after the surrender of the city, when Don Emanuel, accompanied by a constable, turned up in the English camp and demanded that his slave be delivered to him. But the commanding officer informed Don Emanuel that he had lost all right to or property in Cuffee. 'Whereupon', it is said, 'the Spaniard begged pardon for his mistake and walked away'.

Although fewer than 600 men were lost in action on the British side during the siege of Havana, nearly 5000 died from fever or dysentery! On the other hand, the booty taken was enormous. It included over 100 vessels – warships and merchantmen – the total prize-money amounting almost to £750 000. The war ended in February 1763 with the Treaty of Paris, by one of the provisions of which Havana was given back to Spain in exchange for Florida. By the Treaty Britain also secured Dominica, Grenada, and the Grenadines, St Vincent and Tobago.

New developments

An important event in the period covered by this chapter was the arrival, in 1754, of Moravian missionaries in Jamaica, the first denomination to undertake to teach the slaves Christianity. An event of a different kind, but also of far-reaching importance to the island, was the accidental introduction of guinea grass in 1744. A bag of the grass seed was given to Mr George Ellis, twice Chief Justice of Jamaica, as the feed for some rare West African birds brought for him by the captain of a slave ship. The birds died shortly after and the seeds were thrown away in a field where they soon germinated and flourished. Attention was first drawn to the grass by the obvious enjoyment with which the cattle on the property fed on it. Pen-keeping was to benefit greatly from the eventual spread of this grass throughout the island.

Chapter 10

Sugar and slavery

A sugar estate, Jamaica

In almost every chapter so far reference has been made to sugar cane cultivation and to slavery. This is because from the seventeenth century both were central factors in the history of Jamaica, as of the whole West Indies. Besides, both were closely related and went hand in hand. In this chapter we shall trace the story of the two trades, in sugar and in slaves, from their early start to their remarkable rise in value and importance during the second half of the eighteenth century.

The first settlers in the West Indies concerned themselves with tropical crops which could be easily sold in Europe or, later, in North America. They tried tobacco, indigo and cocoa before turning their attention to sugar as the most profitable crop of all. But, for sugar production a large labour force is required and it was out of this need that the African slave trade to the West Indies grew. Another result of this concentration on sugar cane cultivation, far-reaching in its effects, was a change in the social structure of the islands brought about by the disappearance of the small cultivator, as ever larger areas of land came into the hands of the few sugar planters with their armies of black slaves.

The original home of the sugar cane is the South Pacific. Among the ancient legends of that area is one which describes how the first man and woman in the world sprang from two cane shoots. The cane reached Europe by way of India and was introduced by the Spaniards into the New World. From Madeira, where it was planted in 1420, it is said to have been carried by Columbus himself to Hispaniola on his second voyage of discovery, although large scale cultivation was not attempted there till some time later. From Hispaniola sugar cane was doubtless introduced into Jamaica.

The sugar produced here was very small in quantity and was consumed locally. At the time of the English capture of the island, there were only a few sugar works, one of which, in Liguanea, belonged to a rich Spanish widow who, it is said, also owned 40 000 head of cattle.

It was in Barbados, in 1640, that the English first started the systematic cultivation of sugar cane. So profitable was the crop that within ten years the wealth of the planters had multiplied twenty times, and in that time also the slave population had risen from a few hundred to over 20 000.

The capture of Jamaica opened up an area more than twenty-six times that of Barbados, and Sir Thomas Modyford, who was appointed Governor in 1664, promptly set about establishing the sugar industry here on a good footing.

As in Barbados, the rise in production was astonishing. In 1673 there were 57 sugar estates and sixty-six years later there were nearly 430. Sugar had now become the great staple crop of the island and Jamaica was already on the way to becoming the largest English, and – as she was for a time – the largest world producer of sugar.

The Spaniards, and after them the adventurers of all nations, came to the Indies seeking rich mines of gold and silver, but as they were to discover in time, the real wealth of the Indies was the wide fields of sugar cane. In their eighteenth-century heyday the 'sugar colonies', as the islands came to be called, were the most valuable possessions of any empire, fiercely fought over in every war that broke out in Europe and as fiercely bargained for at every peace conference. Their importance in the eyes of governments was out of all proportion to their size: indeed, the British West Indians had more political influence with the government in England than did all thirteen American mainland colonies. Their indignation at the favour shown to these islands was one of the grievances, as will be shown in the next chapter, that led them to revolt against British rule and become an independent republic.

This wealth of the West Indian planters became in time a kind of legend. The large estates were villages in themselves consisting as they did of the overseer's house and offices, the sugar works and mill, boiling house, curing houses and still house, the stables for the grinding cattle, lodging for the white bondsmen, workshops for the smiths, carpenters and coopers, together with the streets of houses for the slaves. On rising ground some distance from the sugar works, the planters usually built their great houses in the elegant style of the day, with finely-cut stone blocks and seasoned timber, handsome carved woodwork and highly polished floors.

The ambition of most planters, however, was not to remain in the West Indies, but to be absentee proprietors, that is, to live in Europe on the profits of their estates and leave the cares and troubles of management to paid attorneys and overseers. Generous, hospitable and hearty, the planters liked to make a great show of their riches, especially when in Europe. Such displays strengthened the belief in the great wealth of the sugar colonies and the expression 'as rich as a West Indian planter' became the accepted description of any very wealthy person.

Sugar was indeed a rich man's business, but as time was to show, not all the planters who cultivated it were rich. The great planter had to be a great land and slave owner as well. In order to make his undertaking profitable he needed large areas of fertile land, a big and expensive labour force, draught animals and equipment – the mill and its furniture, coppers for the boiling house, pots and dips for the cooling house, the still, carts, hoes, cutlasses – to buy which he often had to borrow heavily from merchants in England.

Above all the planter needed labour, for the agricultural and production

Holeing, or placing sugar cane in holes

69

Windmill power was used for grinding the sugar cane

methods of the day were primitive. Large gangs of workers were necessary for the various jobs that had to be done by hand, from the clearing of the brush, the digging of trenches, setting out of the cane shoots, the weeding and harvesting, to the very transporting of the canes to the mill which, in the early days, was done by bearers carrying the loads on their heads. In addition there were the many tasks to be attended to in the factory itself, in the mill, the boiling, curing and still houses. It was this need for manpower which nourished the traffic in slaves until both trades became entirely dependent on each other.

Slavery

Slavery did not originate in the West Indies. It existed from earliest times, and appears in one form or another even today. It was an important part of the social and economic life of all ancient civilisations – of Egypt and Babylon, China and India, Greece and Rome. Nor were Africans the only race to be enslaved: the word *slave* itself comes from the same root as Slav, the name given to the races of eastern Europe who, during the later stages of the Roman Empire, were spread over the continent of Europe in great numbers as slaves. Slavery had also existed among various tribes in Africa, for centuries before the Arabs first began to trade in Africans whom they sold

Interior of a boiling house

in India and Asia. In their footsteps came the Portuguese and, later, other European nations, as the trade in slaves to the New World grew with the rapidly expanding cultivation of the sugar cane.

The early Spanish settlers of the West Indies were accustomed to using slave labour, for from the fifteenth century blacks had been imported from West Africa to work on the estates in southern Spain. It is not surprising, therefore, that black slaves should have been taken over to Hispaniola as early as 1503, and to Jamaica (as well as Puerto Rico, Cuba and the first mainland settlements of Darien) before 1517. These slaves were few in number, however, and had been brought in by individual colonists. Regular large scale importations did not begin until some time later.

The Spaniards also kept the Arawak Indians of the various islands settled by them in a form of slavery, the results of which in Jamaica have already been described. They also tried an experiment of importing labourers from one island to another when they moved the whole Indian population of the Bahamas to Hispaniola to work on the farms and in the mines, but the experiment was not a success. Most of the imported workers died shortly after their arrival from overwork or ill-treatment, or, in despair, committed suicide.

The fate of these people stirred the pity of many of the Spanish clergy in the islands, although themselves slave owners, especially of Bartolomé de las Casas the first Roman Catholic priest to be ordained in the New World. He was moved to recommend that African slaves be purchased from the

Portuguese slave traders and used in Hispaniola and Cuba instead of the Indians. He was later to regret his well-meaning suggestion when he saw the horrible results, even in his time, of the new system.

The first contracts, or *asientos* already referred to, for the large scale supply of slaves to the West Indies were in the hands of the Portuguese who had had long experience in the business, passing later to the Dutch, then to the French, while by the middle of the eighteenth century, with the development of the sugar colonies, the British became the largest West Indian slave dealers.

White Europeans did compulsory labour for a time on West Indian plantations, especially in Barbados, side by side with Africans. These bondsmen, or *indentured servants*, were sent out to the colonies often as political prisoners, but also on occasion because of debt. Some, in desperate search of a living or in hope of picking up a fortune in the islands, came out of their own free will under a contract (or *indenture*) by which they were bound to serve for a fixed period of between three to seven years. Those sent out under sentence of court were usually bound for ten years.

During his period of service the bondsman was regarded as little better than a slave; it is said, in fact, that often he was treated worse than an African would be who, being his owner's property for life, was worth some consideration and care to prolong his usefulness, whereas the bondsman's service was for a limited time during which it was clearly in his master's interest to get the most out of him, to work him to the limit, even to death. Actually on some estates, especially those of absentee proprietors, black slaves were overworked in the same way. In practice the periods of service of most bondsmen lasted much longer than originally agreed upon for the laws at the time provided many years of extra service as the punishment for very minor offences.

This experiment with white forced labour proved unsuccessful and was soon discontinued. It is said that Europeans could not work as long or hard in a tropical climate as could Africans. Besides, the planters found it cheaper to buy a black slave who, together with his children, was his for life, than to purchase for limited periods the services of white bondsmen whose children remained free. So the indentured servant disappeared from the islands as black slaves increased in number, although a certain number of white men continued to be needed on the estates for posts of management and for the more skilled trades of smiths, masons and the like.

In the early days of the slave trade the blacks shipped to the West Indies were mainly prisoners of war or criminals, bought from African chiefs in exchange for European goods; but as the traffic increased the chiefs had to employ different means to maintain the supply. Tribal wars were stirred up for no other reason than the capture of prisoners later to be sold as slaves, stragglers were kidnapped from neighbouring villages for the same purpose, and, with the help of white traders, regular man-hunting raids were organised. The slaves so taken were usually chained or tied to one another and brutally driven down to the coast, a distance often of hundreds of kilometres, where they were stored in 'factories' – large fortified castles especially built for this purpose – until the arrival of the slave ships.

Among the records of the Vice-Admiralty Court, now in the Jamaica

Archives, is a document which describes a man-hunting raid carried out on a fort at the mouth of the Benin River on the Guinea Coast, in 1792. The raiding party consisted of members of the crew of a slave ship named the *Hero* and a number of Africans. The raid was made at the dead of night, the fort set on fire and the surprised villagers captured as they ran in terror from the flames. By six the following morning the raiders had returned to their ship driving before them their unfortunate captives including, as it was later discovered, the daughter of the King of Benin River. Following the usual procedure, the captured blacks were herded aboard the vessel, the members of the raiding party paid off and the *Hero* set sail for the long and dreaded *middle passage* to the West Indies. This passage was so called because the usual voyage of a British slaver was a three-sided one, starting from England with trade goods, to Africa where these were exchanged for slaves; thence to the West Indies where in turn the slave cargo was landed and sugar, rum and molasses taken aboard for the final leg of the journey back to England.

Lasting for anything between six to twelve weeks, the middle passage was perhaps the most dreadful of all the experiences a slave endured. In order to make each trip as profitable as they could, the traders crammed as many slaves aboard their ships as possible. These ships were often quite small sailing craft specially fitted for the traffic by the addition of shelves about one metre apart, attached to the sides between decks. On these shelves the slaves were stacked side by side, chained to one another, without sufficient space in which to sit upright throughout the whole agonising journey. In these conditions it is no wonder that many of the slaves did not survive the middle passage. More than sixteen died on the *Hero* on that trip from Benin before she dropped anchor in Kingston Harbour.

On arrival in port the slaves were put ashore and exhibited to the planters and local dealers to whom they were auctioned. Prices paid varied greatly, but £25–£75 was a usual range. In those days when skilled craftsmen were both scarce and much in demand, a slave trained in a craft always fetched a high price: in the records of the Valley Plantation in the old Parish of St John, for the year 1787, there is an entry showing £330 being paid for a good mill carpenter named Jimmy, while on the same page we find Quamina 'a good watchman, but bad legs' valued at sixpence.

Of the large number of slaves imported into Jamaica during much of the eighteenth century, about 5000 were kept each year in the island, the rest being re-exported, as already explained. The Africans brought in were of many tribes, the majority being Coromantees from the Gold Coast, Eboes from the Bight of Benin and Mandingoes. These people differed greatly in character. As a race, the Coromantees were strong, proud and fierce and were not easily broken to gang labour. They made up the majority of the Maroons and almost every slave revolt was led by Coromantees. The Eboes, on the other hand, had for ages been enslaved in Africa by stronger tribes and were, as a result, docile and rather sad by nature. The women, particularly, made good and willing field labourers.

Besides the difficulty of getting accustomed to plantation life, the newly-arrived slave had also to learn to speak English of a kind. His own language he might use occasionally when conversing with people from his country,

Notice of a sale to take place on 7 October, 1826, of a slave called Phoebe

PHŒBE.

Jamaica Royal Gazette, Oct. 7, 1826.

25—42   Spanish-Town Workhouse.

Notice is hereby given, that unless the undermentioned Slave is taken out of this Workhouse, prior to Monday the 30th day of October next, she will on that day, between the hours of 10 and 12 o'Clock in the forenoon, be put up to Public Sale, and sold to the highest and best bidder, at the Cross-Keys Tavern, in this Town, agreeably to the Workhouse Law now in force, for payment of her fees.

PHŒBE, a Creole, 5 feet 4½ inches, marked NELSON on breasts, and I O on right shoulder, first said to one Miss Roberts, a free Black, in Vere, secondly, to Thomas Oliver, Esq. St. John's, but it is very lately ascertained that her right name is Quasheba, and she belongs to Salisbury-Plain plantation, in St. Andrew's; Mr. John Smith is proprietor.   May 11

Ordered, that the above be published in the Newspapers appointed by Law, for Eight Weeks.

By order of the Commissioners,

T. RENNALLS, Sup.

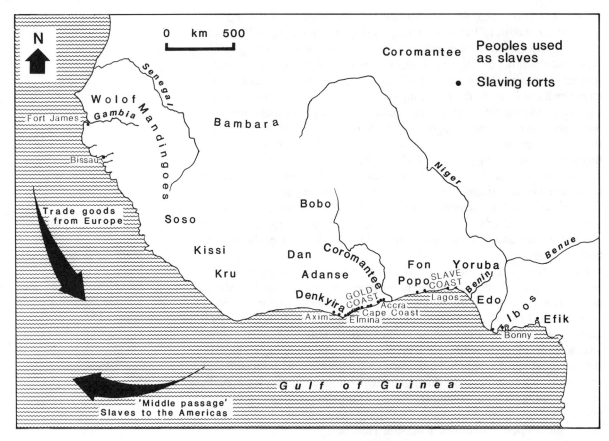

The main sources of African slaves and the ports from which they were shipped

but on any one plantation might be found members of several tribes all speaking different dialects. So, in time the African forgot much of his own language, while the *creole* slaves, that is, those born in the island, knew practically nothing of it. In this way too many of the old beliefs and customs died out or became mixed with those from Europe, producing in time a local dialect and folklore in which both African and European influences mingled freely. Many words still in use today are of African origin, such as *senseh* fowl, from the Ashanti word *asenseh*; or *duckunoo*, *fufu*, *patoo* and *packy*, all from the same dialect. Among Jamaican place names Mocho and Naggos Head are so called after African tribes, while Quaco Bay, Quashie's River and Quao (or Quaw) Hill remind us that the Gold Coast people often named their children according to the days on which they were born: Cudjoe for Monday, Cubbenah for Tuesday, Quaco for Wednesday, Quao for Thursday, Cuffee for Friday, Quamin for Saturday and Quashie for Sunday, the corresponding girl names being Juba, Beneba, Couba, Abba, Phibba, Mimba and Quasheba.

Along with the tribal religions the slaves brought with them from Africa came the peculiar form of witchcraft called *Obeah*, a most harmful force the influence of which added greatly to the miseries of slavery. The power of the obeahman was thought to be unlimited. It was believed that he could cause disease or cure it, punish an enemy or win his favour, detect a thief, a liar or a murderer – all by means of magic spells woven with the aid of such objects as grave dirt, blood, fowls' feet, feathers and teeth. In reality his 'magic' usually consisted of poisons and the fear he was able to inspire in his victims. The obeahmen even claimed to be able to raise a man from the dead or make him invulnerable and some of the most serious slave revolts in the island were encouraged by such promises.

Ironically, the early laws, by forbidding all native religious assemblies, had the effect of encouraging this form of witchcraft since the obeahmen who always worked in secret anyway, were able to continue their trade. Although later outlawed and made punishable by death, the practice of obeah was never successfully stamped out, and its evil influence is still felt even today.

Although the majority of the plantation slaves were predial, or field workers, a number (depending on the size of the place) did domestic duties in the great house and overseer's residence as cooks, maids, butlers, grooms and the like. Generally this service was much lighter than gang labour, and domestic slaves dreaded being transferred to the fields almost more than anything else.

In the field the slaves on sugar plantations were divided into three main groups, the first or 'great gang' consisting of the strongest men and women, cleared the land, dug and planted the sugar canes and in crop time cut the ripe canes or worked in the mill house. The second gang, composed of the bigger boys and girls as well as the old and infirm slaves, did most of the weeding. The third gang consisted of young children who, under the watchful eye and ready switch of some old estate woman, did various light tasks such as tending the gardens and collecting feed for the animals. The two main gangs were under drivers who kept them hard at work with lashes of the cowhide whip, especially in crop time when the mills had to go on rolling day and night.

Punishment was a regular part of estate life and in the early days a planter could do much as he liked with his slaves. In time he came under stricter control as the laws relating to slaves were made less harsh, but the early *slave code*, as it was called, was very brutal. Punishment for what would now be regarded in most cases as minor offences, ranged from death to the cutting off of an arm or leg, and terrible floggings. Revolt was treated as a most serious crime and punished accordingly. Running away from the plantations was a common practice, the penalty for which was also often severe. As late as 1830 – four years only before slavery ended – a slave woman called Congo Nancy was sentenced to life imprisonment at hard labour for escaping from Craig Mill estate in the old parish of St George and staying away for a period exceeding six months.

One reason for the severity of these laws was the belief that only by terrorism and the strictest discipline could the slaves be prevented from rising and killing off their masters whom they outnumbered greatly. This was not true of the slave code only. Discipline in the British Army and Navy, for example, was also very harsh: as late as 1823 an English soldier received 900 lashes of the cat-o'-nine-tails in Jamaica for using rebellious language. The age itself, as we would regard it today, was hard and brutal: in the mid-eighteenth century, for instance, a child in England could be hanged till dead for stealing a handkerchief from anyone.

The imposing facade of Rose Hall Plantation House, Jamaica

Regardless of how harsh the laws were at the time on free men, however, the fact remained that they were free, but the slave was a slave. There was the difference. The lot of a slave depended very much on the nature of his owner. There were bad slave owners, like Annee Palmer of Rose Hall, St James, who is said to have enjoyed torturing her slaves; and others, like Charles Blagrove of Cardiff Hall, St Ann, whose relationship with his slaves was such that by his will he left each one a small gift in recognition of 'their faithful and affectionate service and willing labours'.

Generally too, the more prosperous the plantation, the better the slaves fared. Conditions were also far more satisfactory when the owners ran the properties themselves since the attorneys who acted in their absence were seldom of a type fitted for the responsibility of caring for a large slave population. They were generally too busy to supervise any one plantation properly since they often had the management of several and relied heavily on overseers; besides, they were rarely honest and usually tried to squeeze extra profit out of the plantations for themselves and in doing this the slaves were the main sufferers. The absentee system was basically unsatisfactory: it left the proprietor with the choice of endless wrangling with his paid representatives, or letting his estate slide slowly into bankruptcy.

In Jamaica where land was more plentiful than in most of the other islands, the slaves were given provision grounds on which to grow their own yams, potatoes, plantains and other foodstuffs. They worked on their grounds in the few free hours allowed them, mainly on Saturday afternoons and Sundays (out of crop time) and produced almost all the food they needed, depending on outside sources for salt fish only. The surplus produce they sold in the Sunday markets, earning in this way a little extra money which in time might be sufficient to buy their freedom,[1] and, when free, even to purchase slaves of their own. A slave might also be freed by his owner (and many were) if the latter so wished, either during the owner's lifetime or by his will.

Although the lot of a slave, depending as it did so much on the whims and fancies of others, could often be terrible indeed, there were forces which sometimes fought on his side, among them the early church missionaries. First of these were the Moravians, followed by the Wesleyan Methodists and later the Baptists. They taught the slave Christianity, did what they could to protect him from cruelty and later took part in the struggle for the abolition of slavery itself. Prominent among these early missionaries were George Lisle and Moses Baker, both freed slaves, whose work laid the foundation of the native Baptist churches in Jamaica, and prepared the way for the representatives of the Baptist Missionary Society.

Opportunities for recreation were few, but these the slave learnt to make the most of. There were the Christmas and New Year holidays when the gay and colourful John Canoe (or Jonkonnu) bands roamed the streets, and the teams of pretty Set Girls dressed up in the rich clothes and jewellery of their mistresses competed with one another in the lavishness of their costumes. There were the Easter holidays which, being shorter, were called *pickney Christmas*; and the weekly carnival of the Sunday Markets, chief of which was that held in Kingston where, with noise and merriment amidst thousands of people, pigs, goats, fowls, yams and other vegetables were disposed of, as well as such small home-made articles as mats, baskets, bark ropes, yabbas and jars; and delicacies too, like strawberries grown in the high, cool St Andrew mountains, grapes and melons.

But, apart from these, there were the gatherings at night, when work was over, outside the huts; the singing and the dancing, and the story-telling – stories of Anancy the cunning spider-man; stories of gods and animals, of Africa and its many wonders; stories of longing and despair, and stories of hope.

As we have seen, the slaves did not accept their lot without a struggle. Often this very despair or hope found expression in escape, revolt or suicide. The Maroon Wars and the many uprisings were all bold efforts of resistance, efforts which in time were to have their effect. The eighteenth century that saw some of slavery's grimmest scenes and harshest measures, towards its close saw also some changes for the better, chief of these being a revision of the slave laws which led to improved living and working conditions. These changes were the result largely of the efforts being made in England to secure the abolition of the slave trade, and will be dealt with fully in a later chapter.

[1] Legally, a slave could not own property, but many did.

Chapter 11

Years of crisis

As shown at the end of Chapter 9, the Treaty of Paris brought the Seven Years' War to a victorious close for Britain. Some years of peace were to follow, but, as had happened before, the peace was to prove an uneasy one. The hatred which France and Spain bore Britain and their desire for revenge continued unabated and showed itself in many irritating and aggressive acts. More than once in the ten years that followed the Treaty of Paris, Britain and Spain very nearly went to war. Still the uneasy peace continued, while in America events were building up which were to explode in a revolt of those mainland colonies and a war that won them their independence. The war was to have serious and lasting effects on Jamaica, the period itself to prove one of importance in the island's history.

With the end of the Seven Years' War trade began again to flourish in Jamaica, especially the illicit trade with the Spanish colonies. Stricter enforcement of the various Trade and Navigation Laws soon brought this traffic under some control. In the Assembly disputes again flared up between the governor and assemblymen mainly over the old questions of rights and privileges; and, as had happened before, while this squabbling occupied their time and attention, what might have been a most serious slave revolt broke out in St Mary.

More slave revolts

The plans for the revolt were well laid and, but for the rashness of one of the leaders, might have succeeded. The main plan was to stir up a general uprising during the Christmas holidays, a period when the slaves enjoyed more freedom of movement than usual and when, too, their masters might be expected to have relaxed some of the customary watchfulness and caution. It was later said that an important part of the plot was for the Maroons to come in on the side of the slaves and, with victory, to have shared the country with them, but this may not have been so.

The leaders of the revolt, who were all Coromantees, met secretly in St Mary in July 1765. Before working out their plan of action they first swore a solemn oath of confederacy by drinking from a cup in which rum, gunpowder, graveyard dirt and blood drawn from the arm of each man present were mixed. But the revolt got off to a false start a month before the appointed time when one of the leaders named Blackwell, more eager perhaps than his fellows, gathered some supporters and set fire to the sugar works at Whitehall estate. In the fighting that followed one white man was killed; the rest escaped to Ballard's Valley, pursued by the rebels. Here, an attempt was made to set fire to the house, but the slave who climbed on the roof for this purpose was shot dead and fell to the ground in full view of his fellows, who, growing alarmed, retreated to the woods when the defenders came out of the house to meet them. They were later rounded up and either killed or captured.

The following year another Coromantee uprising, this time in Westmoreland, had to be put down; two years later a plan to destroy Kingston by fire and murder all its inhabitants was revealed by a young slave girl and checked before it could be carried out.

The War of American Independence

While these events were taking place, the clouds of war had begun to gather over America. Briefly, the discontents which were to plunge those colonies into revolt were caused by a series of trade restrictions and taxes imposed by Britain largely in an effort to raise funds for colonial defence and to pay off the debt resulting from the Seven Years' War. One of these restrictions – the Sugar Act, designed to stop trading between the French islands and North America – had been imposed through the influence of the British *sugar colonies*.

Perhaps the most objectionable tax was that levied by the Stamp Act which required all deeds, receipts for money and other legal transactions to be written on stamped paper. Although most of the West Indian colonies[1] quietly paid this tax, rioting mobs in America seized and destroyed the stamped paper sent out from England. As a result of this opposition the Act was repealed, but the spirit of rebellion was now too strong. A boycott of British goods led to what came to be called the 'Boston tea-party' when a number of men disguised as Red Indians boarded some British ships then in port and threw overboard their cargoes of tea. Real trouble started in April 1775 with a skirmish at Lexington Green, not far from Boston; nearly three hundred British soldiers were killed and the War of American Independence had begun.

The West Indian colonies had little or no sympathy with Britain over this war; in fact, the Jamaica House of Assembly expressed its feelings on the subject in a petition to the King, justifying the action of the American colonies and insisting on their right to make their own laws and not to have those made in England forced upon them. The islands knew very well how much they stood to lose by the conflict, and in Jamaica, as elsewhere, alarm

The Battle of Bunker Hill, 17 June, 1795, a major battle in the War of American Independence

[1] The exceptions were St Kitts and Nevis, where rioting broke out.

was soon caused by the threatening attitude of France and Spain who now saw in this war the opportunity of revenge for which they had long waited.

Another cause of anxiety in Jamaica was the dangerous excess in numbers of slaves over the settlers: by 1775 this stood at 200 000 to 12 737. As a result the Assembly passed bills to restrict the importation of slaves, but they were disallowed in England where the trade was regarded as too valuable to be checked or discouraged in any way. Two years later a slave conspiracy in Hanover and Westmoreland was discovered just before the uprising took place. So great was the resulting alarm that a large convoy bound for England was detained for some days until, with the aid of the Navy, peace was restored. Thirty of the ringleaders were executed.

Danger of uprisings came also from the activities of a famous bandit of the period, Jack Mansong, or Three-Fingered Jack[1] as he was better known because of an injury to one of his hands received during a fight with a Scott's Hall Maroon named Quashie. After leading an unsuccessful revolt of the slaves on the plantation to which he belonged, Jack managed to escape to the mountains where, from his hide-outs near Cane River Falls and Mount Lebanus in St Thomas-in-the-East, he terrorised the island by his daring robberies and murders.

He is said to have been over 2 metres tall, amazingly strong, with a long face and fierce black eyes. In addition to a sword and musket, he always carried with him a small Obeah bag which, it was said, made him invulnerable. Certainly the superstitious fear in which he was held helped in the beginning to protect him from harm, despite the offer of a £300 reward by the government for his capture. He was eventually cornered and killed after a terrific fight by Quashie, the same Maroon who had fought him before, and two friends.

The story of Three-Fingered Jack is now part of the island's folklore; there is an old song which describes the general relief at his death:

Beat big drum – wave fine flag:
Bring good news to Kingston Town, O!
No fear Jack's Obeah-bag –
Quashie knock him down, O!

The Maroons themselves proved to be the cause of some concern at this time. As already mentioned, by the terms of their treaty with the government they were required to hand over for trial and punishment any of their number who committed murder, but a mutiny very nearly broke out among them when they were asked to give up a fellow Maroon guilty of a double murder at Old Harbour.

Lewis Hutchinson, the mad owner of Edinburgh Castle, a property in the Pedro district of St Ann, was another disturbing factor at this time. The disappearance of a number of travellers in that area led eventually to the discovery that they had been killed by Hutchinson and their bodies disposed of down a deep sinkhole on the property, still known as

---

[1] Few other persons connected with Jamaica have been the subject of as many publications as Three-Fingered Jack. Many of these, however, are now rare and difficult to consult. Jack's story (and that of Lewis Hutchinson) are told in *Tales of Old Jamaica* by Clinton V. Black. (Collins, London, 1952)

'Hutchinson's Hole.' He was hanged for his crimes in the Spanish Town Parade. The records of his trial are in the Jamaica Archives, and the ruins of his castle may still be seen.

During this time the war went on. At first it did not seem that the Americans could win, but British military reverses towards the end of 1777 changed the course of events and so encouraged the French that within a few months they declared war on Britain. Spain and the Netherlands were to follow two years later.

The main seat of warfare now shifted to the West Indies where a number of islands soon fell to the enemy. The arrival, in the summer of 1779, of the Count d'Estaing at St Domingue with a powerful fleet including transports, led to the belief that Jamaica was now to be invaded, and turned the island 'upside down' as Horatio Nelson expressed it.

Nelson, who was later to become the greatest of all British naval heroes, was in Jamaica at the time waiting for the return of the frigate *Hinchinbrooke* to the command of which he had only recently been promoted. Although a naval officer and still under the age of twenty-one, he was put in charge of the batteries at Fort Charles, Port Royal, manned by 500 men. In a letter to a friend, he describes some of the feverish preparations made to resist the French attack. Five thousand men were encamped between the Ferry and Kingston, a thousand at Fort Augusta and three hundred at the Apostles' Battery. Additional fortifications were thrown up on all sides, existing forts repaired and strengthened and trees felled and used as roadblocks.

But all these preparations, as well as the skilful disposition of the few warships then in port, did not reassure Nelson, who doubted that the island could successfully resist the attack. Up and down the platform of Fort Charles (now known as Nelson's Quarterdeck) he paced, watching for the first signs of the French fleet. Today a marble tablet fixed to the wall commemorates his association with the old fort:

Viscount Horatio Nelson, English admiral

IN THIS PLACE DWELT HORATIO NELSON.
You who tread his footprints
Remember his glory.

The invasion did not come, after all. The Count d'Estaing later sailed for North America and the arrival at Jamaica of naval reinforcements relieved the fear and tension which had gripped the island. But the respite was to be short-lived: other threats soon developed.

With Spain now in the war, fighting broke out in Central America where the British settlements were being raided. Early in 1780 an expedition, planned by Colonel John Dalling, then Lieutenant-Governor of Jamaica, was sent from the island to Nicaragua. The object was for the British to take Fort San Juan on the river of that name which flows from Lake Nicaragua into the Caribbean, to make themselves masters of the lake itself and of the cities of Granada, and of León on the Pacific side. The plan, if successful, could have been far-reaching in its effects as it would have resulted in the cutting of Spanish communications between their northern and southern possessions in America.

The expedition which was convoyed by Nelson in the *Hinchinbrooke*,

George Brydges Rodney, 1st Baron Rodney, British admiral

achieved some success at first, largely through his activity, but disaster followed with an outbreak of fever amongst the troops. More than two-thirds of the force perished in the swamps. Nelson himself caught the fever, having been poisoned as well by manchineel, and on the return to Port Royal was so weak that he had to be carried ashore in his cot. He was taken to the lodging house run by the popular coloured proprietress Couba Cornwallis, who nursed him tenderly. She often looked after the naval officers on the station and was much loved. Nelson later went to the Admiral's country residence in St Andrew, but there the dullness of life and inactivity soon began to make him fret, and in a letter to one of his friends he exclaimed, 'Oh, what would I give to be at Couba's lodgings at Port Royal!' Couba was later to care also for Prince William who became William IV, the 'Sailor-King', when he visited the island (the first member of the Royal Family to do so) as a young midshipman.

In March 1780, Admiral George Rodney took over the command of the British fleet and around the same time Rear-Admiral de Guichen came out as commander of the French. Although both fleets met more than once soon after, the actions were not decisive. With Spain's entry into the war in June, a Spanish fleet with transports carrying 10 000 men (intended for an attack on Jamaica or some other British island), arrived at Martinique; but sickness among the troops hindered the project. The Spanish admiral withdrew to Havana, de Guichen returned to Europe, and Rodney, who had been watching their movements carefully, now sailed for North America to reinforce the British fleet there and also to remove his ships from the Caribbean during the hurricane season – a shrewd precaution for, as it happened, he escaped some of the most destructive of all West Indian hurricanes.

Jamaica was struck on 3 October, Barbados and the neighbouring islands a week later. In Jamaica the south-western part of the island suffered most, Savanna-la-Mar being completely destroyed. Here is the account of the hurricane given by the Governor, Colonel John Dalling, in his official report to London:

On Monday the 2^d Ins! the weather being very close, the sky on a sudden became very much overcast, & an uncommon elevation of the sea immediately followed – whilst the unhappy Settlers at Savanna-la-Mar were observing this extraordinary Phenomenon, the sea broke suddenly in upon the town, and on its retreat swept every thing away with it, so as not to leave the smallest vestige of Man, Beast, or House behind – This most dreadful catastrophe was succeeded by the most terrible hurricane that ever was felt in this Country with repeated shocks of an earthquake, which has almost totally demolished every building in the parishes of Westmoreland, Hanover, part of St James's and some part of St Elizabeth's.

Rivers changed their courses, lakes were formed, roads blocked for miles and crops utterly destroyed, including all the slaves' provision grounds. Famine followed and epidemics soon broke out. But Jamaica was not the only sufferer. In Barbados more than 4300 people died in the hurricane there, in Martinique fully 7000, and on almost every West Indian beach bits of wrecked vessels – British, French and Spanish – sprawled on the soft sands.

In August the following year another hurricane, scarcely less violent, struck Jamaica. Over a hundred ships were driven ashore, including a number of men-o'-war, and again all the newly-planted provision grounds were destroyed. In February of that year Rodney had captured the Dutch island of St Eustatius, or 'Statia' as it was familiarly known – a great Caribbean trade centre and the chief source of military supplies for the American colonies. A hundred and fifty loaded merchantmen were taken in the harbour and £3 000 000 worth of produce on shore! The following month the Dutch South American colonies of Demerara, Essequibo and Berbice (later called British Guiana and now the Cooperative Republic of Guyana) fell to Rodney, but the French under Admiral de Grasse made a successful attack on Tobago, and under de Bouillé recaptured St Eustatius.

Meanwhile in America the colonists, aided now by French troops and ships, were fast turning the tide of war. In October the British forces under General Cornwallis surrendered to General Washington at Yorktown, Virginia. The War of American Independence was almost at an end, but the last battles were yet to be fought . . . in West Indian waters.

The Battle of the Saints

In 1782 all seemed lost. Only Jamaica, Barbados and Antigua were left in British hands, but de Grasse was determined that they should not remain

Battle of the Saints, 12 April, 1782

83

so. He decided to join forces with the Spanish and invade Jamaica. Nothing, it seemed, could prevent him – except perhaps Rodney and his fleet, lurking now off the northern tip of St Lucia at Gros Islet Bay, and keeping close watch on Fort-de-France in neighbouring Martinique where the French ships lay at anchor.

Meanwhile in Jamaica preparations were being made for a stubborn land resistance, in case the Navy failed. Extra taxation was imposed to meet the cost of large scale defensive preparations as once more forts were manned and the militia called up. Amidst the general confusion caused by these measures, a fire broke out in Kingston which, but for the fortunate shifting of the wind, would probably have burnt the city to the ground. As it was, property to the value of nearly £1 000 000 was destroyed.

Slowly the days lengthened to weeks, weeks of uncertainty and dread, weeks of waiting, for there was no way of knowing what was happening outside the island; nor did Rodney have time to send word that de Grasse had shipped out of Fort-de-France and that he and his fleet were in close pursuit. Battle was at length joined on 12 April and by the masterly manœuvre of breaking the enemy's line Rodney scored a decisive victory off a group of islets between Dominica and Guadeloupe known as the Saints, from which the battle got its name.

It is said the enemy were so certain the engagement would be no more than a brush, that to prepare for action they did not even remove the live oxen crowding the decks of several of their ships. Many of the oxen, stung to madness by their wounds and the noise of the cannon, broke loose, adding greatly to the dismay and confusion of the French.

At sunset de Grasse struck his flag. The day was won and the threatened invasion of Jamaica prevented. The island went almost wild with joy at the news of victory, and again when Rodney arrived with his fleet and the captured French vessels – the English colours flying above their own – including the splendid enemy flagship *Ville de Paris* of over 100 guns, and Admiral de Grasse himself as prisoner.

Days and nights for weeks on end Jamaica fêted the victors and celebrated victory, and for years after, no ball or play was thought complete unless this triumph was recalled. The Assembly decided that the event should be commemorated by the erection of a marble statue of Lord Rodney, and John Bacon the famous sculptor was eventually given the job. The Assembly voted £1000 for the statue, but the cost when completed, plus that of the *temple* to contain it, of the land and of the erection of the public offices which stand on either side amounted almost to £31 000.

It is interesting to note that Spanish Town very nearly lost the memorial to the rival claim of Kingston. As soon as news was received that the statue was on its way from England, the people of Kingston and of Port Royal petitioned the House of Assembly that it might be placed in the Kingston Parade, set in the centre of a spacious water-filled basin which they proposed to build. The Assembly divided equally on the question and only the vote of the Speaker tipped the scale in Spanish Town's favour.

Two finely-decorated, hand-finished cannon, taken from the French flagship, now stand on either side of the statue as symbols of the spoils of war. It is fortunate that they were deposited here before Rodney sailed for

England with his prizes, for on the way the convoy ran into a violent Atlantic storm which sent the *Ville de Paris*, and another vessel *Le Glorieux*, to the bottom with the loss of 1200 men.

Rodney's victory – the only gleam of sunshine in the whole miserable war – not only saved Jamaica from invasion and almost certain capture, but restored British prestige, badly lowered by the success of the American revolution, and enabled Britain to secure more favourable terms under the Treaty of Versailles which formally brought the war to an end in September, 1783. Britain's only loss in the West Indies was the small island of Tobago, which, anyway, was recovered later.

The war proved disastrous even to the few islands, like Jamaica, which were not invaded by the enemy. The almost constant threat of attack made martial law frequently necessary, throwing a great physical strain on the militia and a financial burden on the islands' resources from which the expense of defensive measures had largely to be met.

Jamaica, in company with the other sugar islands, depended heavily on North America for supplies of corn and flour for the white colonists, and of salt-fish for the slaves; as well as for supplies of staves and hoops from which sugar hogsheads were made, and timber, boards and shingles. With the outbreak of war these supplies were cut off, while the other commerce of the islands was hindered by American privateers even before France and Spain entered the war. As a result the price of imports rose steeply, while that of the main exports – sugar and rum – fell.

In Jamaica alone, between 1780 and 1787, the cutting off of food supplies, coupled with the repeated destruction by hurricanes of the provision grounds, resulted in the death mainly from starvation of some 15 000 slaves. One effect of this was a desperate search for additional food crops to help feed the island's large labour force.

The introduction of new plants

Two plants of great economic value introduced during the war were the ackee, from West Africa in 1778, and the mango, four years later. The first ackee slips were purchased from the captain of a slaver, while the first mango seedlings to reach Jamaica were part of a collection sent to the French West Indian islands from Mauritius at the command of the French government. The vessel carrying the plants was captured by one of Lord Rodney's ships. The Admiral himself, recognising the potential value of the captured plants to Jamaica, sent them here where they were successfully grown at the botanical garden kept by Hinton East at Gordon Town.

The peace treaty which recognised the United States as an independent country, created serious problems for the British West Indies, especially in connection with trade. Petitions to London from Jamaica and the other islands for a resumption of trade with the United States on the old terms were, not unnaturally, refused. By declaring and winning their independence, the United States were now a foreign power with which British colonies might trade under certain conditions only, as laid down by law.

William Bligh, British admiral

These provided that British West Indian sugar, rum, molasses, coffee and pimento could be exported to the United States on the same terms as to another British colony; flour, bread, grain, timber and livestock could be imported from the United States, but in British ships only; while United States meat and fish could not be imported at all. These supplies, on which the island relied heavily, had now to come from Canada, Nova Scotia, Newfoundland, or England, at higher prices (at least in the beginning) and in smaller quantities than they used to from America. Fortunately, as we shall see, the governors of the West Indian islands were allowed to use their judgment in the matter and to permit freer trading if this proved necessary.

In July 1784, Jamaica was struck by a violent hurricane. Among the buildings blown down were the barracks at Up-Park Camp, and as usual, many lives were lost and almost all ships in Kingston Harbour were either sunk or driven ashore. Damage done to plantations and growing crops was most serious; as a result the island was faced with starvation and the Governor, within a month of the hurricane, was to permit for a time the importation of provisions from foreign sources and in foreign ships. The following year another hurricane struck the island and yet another the year after. The terrible effects of these disasters on the island's food supplies have already been mentioned, as well as the strong action taken by the government to solve the problem of growing new forms of cheap starch for feeding the large number of slaves employed in the fields.

In 1791 the Jamaica Assembly resolved to give every encouragement to the cultivation of yams, cocos, maize, plantains and such products as the nutmeg, cloves, cinnamon and coffee, since it believed that the cultivation of these crops would be of benefit to the island in many ways, while making it less dependent on America for food and other supplies. The encouragement had its effect: in a short time nutmeg and coffee became almost as important export crops as pimento and cocoa, although none rivalled sugar in value.

The breadfruit was first brought to Jamaica by Captain William Bligh in 1793 from the Pacific island of Tahiti. Six years before, Bligh had been sent, in command of H.M.S. *Bounty*, to the Pacific to collect food and vegetable plants with a view to their being cultivated in the West Indies, but his crew mutinied and he and eighteen men who remained loyal to him were set adrift in an open boat in which they were to sail some 6000 kilometres before reaching land.

The breadfruit trees (as well as the otaheite apple and jack-fruit, amongst others) which Bligh eventually brought to the island, were planted in the Botanical Gardens at Bath, St Thomas-in-the-East, and from there distributed over the island. Actually, the Jamaica slaves refused to eat the breadfruit because it did not resemble any food plant to which they had been accustomed in Africa or the West Indies. So, as it happened, for fifty years breadfruit was fed to pigs, nor was it until after the abolition of slavery that it became an important source of food for the free peasant communities.

Chapter 12

Effects of the French Revolution

Two events of worldwide importance were beginning to have their effect on Jamaica, the anti-slavery movement in England and the French Revolution. The story of the Revolution is a long one and cannot be told here in any detail. It may be said to have started on 14 July 1789, when a mob in Paris, imbued with the ideals of the rights of man and the stirring concept of, 'Liberty! Equality! Fraternity!' attacked and captured the terrible prison of the Bastille. The Revolution which had been brewing for a long time, sprang from a desperate desire on the part of the people of the country to throw off the oppressive rule of the king and his government. It was a revolution which was to have a deep and far-reaching effect, not only on the story of France but on the modern history of all Europe and on that of much of the New World as well.

St Domingue

At first the French West Indian islands did not understand clearly what was happening in France. Events were confused and the news of them took long to arrive, but St Domingue, more alert than the smaller islands, seemed to realise early that great things were in the air. It was in this island – France's largest and richest colony, and the nearest to Jamaica – that the Revolution was to have its most violent and lasting effect.

Even when the events then taking place in France were more clearly understood, the reaction in the French islands was disordered. This is understandable when one considers how the population of these islands was composed. In France the struggle was one between two groups – the people and the aristocrats who oppressed them. But in St Domingue at that time the population consisted of a number of groups, the three main ones, all antagonistic to one another, were the white colonists, the free mulattoes and the great numbers of slaves. The *creole* or local-born slaves looked with scorn on the newly-imported Africans; the creoles in turn were despised by the fair-skinned mulattoes who, with the others, were in their turn despised by the whites. It is easy to understand the utter confusion into which a society like this would be thrown by an upheaval such as the French Revolution, which was guided by the belief that all men were free, brothers and equal.

In St Domingue the free mulattoes were the first to take advantage of what was happening in France to demand full civil liberties. These were granted to them, only to be withdrawn shortly afterwards. The resentment which this naturally caused came to a head on 28 October 1790, with a revolt led by a wealthy young mulatto named Ogé. Ogé, who was educated in Paris, had become a member of a society called *Les Amis des Noirs* – 'Friends of the Blacks' – from whom he learnt the new teaching of equality and the rights of man. Convinced that he was destined to free the coloured people of his native island from the wrongs and abuses they had to bear, he returned secretly to St Domingue and started a revolt. After some early successes he and his small force were defeated in their first clash with regular troops and militia. Ogé and his principal followers escaped to the Spanish part of the island, but were captured and handed over to the French authorities. Most were either executed or imprisoned, Ogé himself being broken on the wheel. In this form of torture and execution the victim was tied to a cart-wheel which had been placed on its side, or to a cross-shaped wooden frame, and his bones broken with blows from an iron bar. The torture over, a heavy blow on chest or stomach usually ended the victim's suffering.

The suppression of this revolt only fanned the flames of hatred of mulatto for white. And, all the while, the first warning signs of unrest among the slaves went unnoticed until August when, at a given signal, the slaves of the northern plain rose in revolt, setting fire to the canefields and houses and murdering the white inhabitants. One of the earliest leaders was Boukman who is said to have been a slave in Jamaica.

At first only a few plantations were involved, but the rising spread rapidly. Armed with any weapons on which they could lay hands, the slaves rose in ever-growing numbers, soon overwhelming the few thousand white colonists and the handful of regular soldiers who opposed them. More than 12 000 people were killed in the first two months of savage fighting, and 180 sugar plantations destroyed. It was August and the fields of cane blazed furiously, the flames spreading to the coffee estates on the mountain slopes and to the indigo settlements, until the whole country seemed alight. The fierce glow of the fires was seen for many kilometres out to sea, and the ashes carried by the wind fell even on Jamaica. Thousands were to die and much of the country was to be laid waste in this great and terrible revolution when the white population of the French part of the island was wiped out and the black republic of Haiti was born.

The effect on Jamaica

These events naturally had a marked effect on life in Jamaica. From the beginning there was fear that the spirit of revolution might spread to the slaves here for there was no hiding the news from them. Refugees fleeing for their lives were pouring into the island, bringing those of their own slaves who had remained faithful and from whom, if from no other source, the Jamaican slaves were certain to hear of what was taking place only a 150 kilometres away.

This flow of refugees and later of French prisoners of war was itself a danger to the security of the island since it gave an opportunity for spies and agents of the revolution to enter unnoticed and stir up disorder. As a result, a very strict watch was kept, the militia was called up for guard duty and warships with troops on board were stationed off the coast as a further precaution.

A serious outbreak of trouble among the Trelawny Town Maroons in 1795 (dealt with in the following chapter), which completely disorganised the life of the island for a time, is said to have been encouraged by French agents. This may or may not have been so, but four years later plots to stir up revolts in the island and so prepare the way for an invasion were discovered, as a result of which two spies, Duboison and Sas Portas, were caught and a number of refugees and their slaves on whom suspicion fell deported. Duboison saved himself by giving evidence against his comrades in return for a pardon, but Sas Portas was hanged for his part in the affair on the Kingston Parade.

A slave uprising, which in the state of fear that gripped the island probably seemed more dangerous than in fact it was, and a disastrous fire that almost destroyed the then thriving town of Montego Bay, added to the general state of alarm. An attempt, shortly before, to set fire to Kingston, no doubt encouraged the belief that the destruction of Montego Bay was deliberate, but according to one account the fire started when sparks from a forge caught a pile of straw stacked nearby. The flames spread rapidly to wharves and warehouses and were only checked when the court house building was blown up to create a fire brake.

It must also be mentioned, however, that the majority of the St Domingue refugees who remained on the island settled satisfactorily into the community, the government and private people subscribing generously towards their support. Nor did their arrival bring gloom only: a few of them were actors and professional entertainers who helped to brighten life by their performances at the Kingston Theatre – like Monsieur du Mulin, for example, whose main act was a dance on the tight rope with two children tied to his feet!

For the first four years of the French Revolution Britain did not interfere, nor was Jamaica, although close to St Domingue, officially involved in events there, except in the following minor ways. Shortly after the revolt broke out in that island, two commissioners came to Jamaica seeking help for the whites in their fight against the slaves. The government voted a small sum of money and the Kingston merchants helped by giving them considerable credit. The governor, Major-General Adam Williamson, also sent a few warships to Cap François to pick up refugees. But apart from this there was no interference in the affairs of St Domingue, although the white colonists there, especially those of the southern peninsula who had so far managed to hold their own, urged Britain to occupy the country, promising their loyalty and support. The situation suddenly changed, however, when in January 1793 the French king, Louis XVI, was executed on the guillotine and Britain and most of the European nations went to war with France. The Governor of Jamaica was now ordered to send an invading force to help suppress the revolution, rescue the colonists and occupy the country; while across the border, in Santo Domingo, the Spanish prepared to launch a similar attack.

The British force consisted of some 900 soldiers, later reinforced from England, and by slave regiments raised in Jamaica. Commanded by Colonel John Whitelocke, the army sailed from Port Royal in September and landed without opposition at Jérémie near the tip of the southern peninsula, where they were warmly welcomed by the white colonists. Within two days Môle St Nicolas on the northern peninsula was taken. Léogane and other coastal towns also fell, but at Tiburon difficulties began. With the help of reinforcements from England the town was taken, but yellow fever broke out and as many soldiers were killed by it as by war.

Soon it became clear that events were not going according to plan. Reinforcements were slow in coming and too few in number, the Maroon trouble in Jamaica delayed the arrival of troops at a time when they were badly needed, in addition the support promised by the white colonists had not been forthcoming. Apart from these factors, the upheaval which had started as a slave revolt had now become a formidable national rising led by one of the most outstanding black men who ever lived, the former slave François-Dominique Toussaint (soon to become known as L'Ouverture, 'The Opening', because of his reported success on one occasion in opening a gap in the ranks of the enemy), the first of a remarkable series of black Haitian leaders.

With a force of some 20 000 men, Toussaint, commanding in the north, successfully prevented the invaders from making their way inland. The British eventually captured Port-au-Prince and many ships in the harbour, but losses in the fighting and from fever made the victory hardly worthwhile. In May 1795, General Williamson himself went over to take command of the troops. He was knighted before he left and given the title of 'Governor of St Domingue' – an empty title, for the country was far from conquered. In fact, despite the troops now being thrown into the fight, including more Jamaican black regiments, the coastal towns were being recaptured one by one, as the fever did its deadly work, a whole regiment, the 96th, perishing to a man.

And so the wasting war went on. In 1798 Brigadier-General Thomas Maitland, then in command of the British forces, found himself unable to continue the struggle. Pressed now on all sides, his small force could no longer hold out against the enemy. In England a decision was even then being taken to send out fresh troops to continue the fight, but Maitland knew nothing of this and probably could not have held out even if he did. In April he made terms with Toussaint (who promised, among other things, not to molest British trade) and withdrew to Jamaica with the remnants of the army. The black troops he disbanded and left in St Domingue since it was felt that after what they had seen they might come back and start a revolution in Jamaica. Most of them joined Toussaint's army.

Toussaint L'Ouverture, the Haitian revolutionary leader

And there we must leave the story of St Domingue, except to say that with the British out of the way, Toussaint soon took control of the country. Of his two most active helpers, Dessalines and Henri Christophe, both slaves like himself, the former succeeded him as leader and continued the struggle to such good effect that in 1803 the French evacuated the island, never to return, although 23 years were to pass before France fully recognised the Haitian Republic.

The international struggle which started with the Revolutionary War, and in which the French and British were to be the main combatants, did not end till 1815. Although the famous battles, like those of Trafalgar and Waterloo, were fought in Europe, the Caribbean was nevertheless, as usual, the scene of heavy fighting, in which Britain enjoyed the advantage because

The statue on National Heroes Circle, Kingston, of Simon Bolivar, the South American soldier and liberator

of her naval superiority. Islands were captured, only to be retaken or later restored. The peace treaties by which the war ended, assigned to Britain the French islands of Tobago and St Lucia, and the three Dutch provinces making up what is now Guyana. With this arrangement British possessions in the West Indies were finally settled.

The period saw the return of Lord Nelson to these waters. In 1805 the news that a French fleet was on its way to Jamaica resulted in the proclaiming of martial law and, among other precautions, the removal of the island's archives to the church in St Thomas-in-the-Vale for safe keeping under militia guard. The fleet never managed to carry out its intended attack, being eventually driven from these waters by Nelson. Admiral Duckworth's brilliant victory over a French squadron the following year off St Domingue gladdened the hearts of all in Jamaica, especially of the people of Kingston who, three years earlier, had had another good cause to rejoice when their town received its charter as a city.

In March 1808, the Duke of Manchester arrived as governor. His term of office, which lasted nearly twenty years, is the longest on record. It covered an important period in the history of the island. It was during his governorship that Simón Bolivar, the great revolutionary leader who was to free South America from Spanish rule, visited Jamaica . . . and nearly lost his life. Pio, his black servant, was bribed by Spanish agents to murder him. But in the darkness one night Pio stabbed to death a man who was lying in Bolivar's hammock at the time.

In spite of the anxieties and difficulties of the revolutionary years, the long war brought many economic benefits to Jamaica and the British West Indian islands. St Domingue before the slave uprising was producing nearly as much sugar as all the British islands combined; with production brought to a standstill there, the gain to the British was tremendous. Sugar prices rose and that of coffee doubled as Jamaican exports of both products increased greatly. The war with the United States, known as the War of 1812, which broke out during this period, also brought benefits to Jamaica in the form of increased trade with Cuba and Latin America.

But these wartime advantages were not lasting. They were destined to end even before peace came. For one thing, most West Indians believed that sugar could not be produced without slaves. But as we shall see later an Act of Parliament in 1807 had made the slave trade illegal for British subjects, while Cubans, for instance, could import all the slaves they wished. What was more, with the peace West Indian planters knew that the anti-slavery organisations would begin to press for emancipation itself. After the prosperity of the war years, the future suddenly seemed bleak.

Chapter 13

The Second Maroon War

The outbreak among the Trelawny Town Maroons in July 1795, threw the island into a state of alarm. Had this disturbance occurred at almost any other time in the country's history it might not have ended as sadly as it did, but with the example of what was happening in St Domingue clearly before them, the people of Jamaica feared an uprising at that moment more than almost anything else. The result was the Maroon trouble came to be magnified into a *war* and was dealt with as such.

Of the five permanent settlements established after the First Maroon War, only that of Trelawny Town was involved in the outbreak; the neighbouring people of Accompong refused to join their comrades; they later helped to fight against them. The cause of the trouble was said to be the flogging in Montego Bay of two Trelawny Town Maroons for pig-stealing; but other factors played a part, the chief being a dislike of Captain Craskell, the white superintendent recently stationed in the settlement, and discontent with the original grant of land made to them.

James, the previous superintendent, had been for long a great favourite. If he had been born a Maroon he could not have been more like one. In every respect he lived the life they did, even to roaming barefooted with them over the rough Cockpit country and hunting the wild boar. Strong and fearless, he thought nothing of braving the flashing cutlasses of the Maroons whenever a fight broke out among them, and stopping further trouble simply by knocking down the fighters and clapping them in irons. He was their chief adviser and friend, he settled their accounts for labour, decided disputes and protected them from being taken advantage of by outsiders. Craskell's manner and methods were different and the Maroons had made up their minds to have James back, although they themselves had been largely responsible for his removal.

The flogging of the two Maroons, carried out under sentence of court, was not in itself objected to by the Trelawny Town people. It was the fact that the black workhouse driver who wielded the whip, and most of the prisoners who were allowed to look on and mock, were runaway slaves whom the Maroons had previously caught and handed over to the authorities for punishment. This was an unbearable insult and when news of it reached Trelawny Town there was an instant uproar. Wild threats of vengeance were made against the people of Montego Bay, and Captain Craskell was ordered to leave the settlement forthwith. Alarmed by these proceedings the magistrates asked for a detachment of mounted troops to reinforce the local militia who only numbered about 400 at the time. And so were the first steps taken in this tragic episode.

As the first wave of anger died down somewhat, the Maroons asked for an opportunity to discuss their complaints with the authorities. Accordingly the Custos and other prominent people of the parish went up to Trelawny Town for this purpose. They found the Maroons prepared to listen to reason, and after hearing their complaints promised to lay them before the Governor, to recommend their favourite superintendent be reappointed and that they be given extra land. Reassured by these promises, the Maroons said they had nothing more to ask.

The Earl of Balcarres who had recently arrived as governor took a serious view of the matter. Himself a soldier and veteran of the War of American Independence, he believed in strong measures, especially in this case for he was convinced that the real origin of the Maroon unrest was connected with the revolution then raging in nearby St Domingue. It has, in fact, been suggested that the Maroons were encouraged to revolt by French secret agents. Balcarres feared that a Maroon disturbance might spread to the slaves: indeed it was rumoured that the Maroons were trying to make the slaves join with them in a general uprising. If this were true, then they had little or no success; perhaps the slaves were unwilling to side with people who had so far helped to crush their own revolts, and who for cash hunted and handed over runaways to the government authorities.

Nevertheless, for a time it seemed that the Maroon trouble would be settled peacefully; but rumours continued to reach Balcarres that confirmed his fears and convinced him the Maroons were really determined on a fight but were only waiting for the most favourable moment at which to strike. This gave him the excuse he wanted. Martial law was declared and the militia called out. Most of the regular troops in the island had by this time been sent to St Domingue, and the only remaining regiment was even then on its way to join forces there where it was badly needed. The transports carrying these troops had sailed from Port Royal on 29 July when Balcarres decided to recall them. He sent a fast sailing boat, fitted also with oars for rowing at night when the wind dropped, which caught up with the transports off the north-east end of the island and safely delivered his orders to alter course and proceed instead to Montego Bay.

Balcarres took over command of all the forces and set out himself for Montego Bay. At Llandovery near St Ann's Bay he was met by six Maroon captains, then on their way to Spanish Town to present their grievances in person. He promptly had them imprisoned. Older residents who had had long experience in dealing with the Maroons begged the Governor to be calmer and more patient in his handling of the situation, but he was determined to use his own methods.

From his headquarters he next sent a message to the Maroons telling them that they were surrounded by thousands of troops and giving them four days in which to surrender to him, otherwise they would be attacked and their town destroyed. The Maroons were no doubt alarmed by this order and uncertain what to do about it. The older people of the settlement were strongly in favour of surrendering, but the younger men would not agree to do so. The Governor's harsh terms might have angered them: it was not for nothing that their ancestors had fought so hard for the independence they now enjoyed. Besides, they were naturally suspicious and wondered what their fate would be when they surrendered, pointing to what had been done to the six captains at Llandovery.

In the end only 38 surrendered, led by their aged chief Montague, dressed in his gaudy red coat and gold-laced plumed hat. On their arrival at Vaughan's Field where the Governor had set up his headquarters, they were arrested, tied up and later sent on to Montego Bay to prison. Two of their number only were allowed to return to Trelawny Town with instructions to advise the others to surrender also, but their report had the opposite effect. The Maroons immediately set fire to their town and withdrew into the hills with their women and children.

Balcarres ordered a detachment of men to march inland and destroy the settlement's provision grounds, but on arrival they found that the Maroons had already done so and had disappeared. On the return march, while going through a narrow mountain pass, the detachment was caught in an ambush. Using their favourite method of fighting from cover, the Maroons, cleverly hidden behind rocks and trees, fired volley after volley into the line of soldiers, killing the colonel in charge as well as a number of officers and men and wounding many more. Thrown into disorder by this deadly fire which seemed to come from an invisible enemy, the survivors lost heart and fled from the scene.

With this skirmish the Second Maroon War commenced, a war in which

A Maroon ambush on Dromilly Estate

a mere 300 or so hardy mountain people were to hold out for more than five months against 1500 chosen European troops and more than twice that number of local militia, helped to some extent by the Accompong Maroons. In the wild and almost impenetrable Cockpits where most of the fighting took place, the white troops were no match for the Maroons who, by their cunning and knowledge of the country, were able to draw their attackers time and again into ambushes and slaughter them with hardly any losses on their side. All attempts to drive the Maroons out of their hiding places proved useless. On one occasion the forests in the neighbourhood of their town were cleared by a gang of one thousand slaves, then guns were brought up and the interior shelled. The Maroons merely withdrew and appeared again higher up the hills.

So the war dragged on with the Maroons growing steadily bolder with each success. They began to raid outlying plantations, murdering the planters and their families and carrying off the slaves. Catadupa, Lapland and Mocha were among the properties burnt in such raids, and many others were attacked. Gradually the whole life of the island was disrupted by the war. Jamaica, as one writer of the time expressed it, seeming 'more like a garrison . . . than a country of commerce and agriculture'.

It was at this stage that General George Walpole was placed in command of the forces. His appointment brought about some marked changes. He had a chain of armed posts built along the mountains, from which rapid advances could be made into Maroon country without the necessity of long, tiring marches. He also trained the troops how to fight more effectively in that type of terrain. As a result the Maroons were now kept on the move and slowly pushed farther and farther away from their sources of food and water, until it seemed that they must either surrender or die in the woods. Although hard pressed they were far from beaten, as soon became evident when a Maroon captain named Johnson managed to lead a small party of his men into St Elizabeth and set fire to plantations there.

In spite of his successes General Walpole knew full well that he was up against a tough enemy. After many weary weeks of tracking and marching through the tangled forests he once wrote in a letter to the Governor that there was 'little chance of any but a Maroon discovering a Maroon'. But the Governor and Council were even then considering another method of fighting the Maroons – with the aid of bloodhounds. They knew that the use of these savage dogs would be condemned – as it was by the government of Britain – but felt the seriousness of the situation justified their action.

A militia colonel named William Dawes Quarrell was commissioned to secure a supply of these animals from Cuba where they were in common use for hunting runaway slaves and robbers. He returned to Montego Bay on 14 December with a shipload of 100 dogs and 40 handlers, known as *chasseurs*. These chasseurs were strong, hardy men, accustomed to great exertion and to living in the woods for long periods on very little food. They wore loose check trousers and shirt, a broad-brimmed straw hat and shoes of untanned leather; all carried a heavy cutlass, sharpened like a razor, attached to a stout belt. Fastened by strong ropes to the belt were their dogs – two to each man. The dogs were big, fierce, broad-chested brutes, well trained to their work.

Dogs and men were moved up country without delay where they were met by General Walpole. While inspecting them a musket salute was fired which so excited the animals that, dragging the chasseurs with them, they dashed towards the General who had to run for his life. He barely reached the safety of his carriage in time: as it was, the horses narrowly escaped being torn to pieces! Another example of the ferocity of these animals was provided a few hours later when a woman who was cooking a meal out in the open, unwisely struck at one of the dogs which, happening to be loose at the time, had tried to snatch a bit of the meat. The dog caught her instantly by the throat, and refused to let go his hold until a chasseur was forced to cut his head off, but too late to save the woman's life.

A chasseur with his two dogs

The news of the dogs' arrival caused a panic among the Maroons. In the wild and trackless Cockpits these men had shown that they could elude almost any number of troops which might be sent against them, but they knew there was no escape from bloodhounds who tracked by scent and would in time discover them wherever they might hide. General Walpole was most unwilling to use the dogs and gave the Maroons the chance of surrendering, which they took, on the understanding made with him that they would not be executed or transported from the island. They, on their part, agreed to seek His Majesty's pardon for their revolt, to settle on whatever lands the Governor, Council and Assembly might think fit to allow them, and to deliver up all runaway slaves, about 100 of whom had joined them during the revolt.

This agreement, made on 21 December, was confirmed by the Governor a week later and 1 January fixed as the day on which all the Maroons were to surrender to him. But it was impossible for the surrender to be completed in three days. For one, a much longer time was needed in which to collect together the women and children, scattered as they were in hiding places all over the hills, and an outbreak of measles among the children added to the delay. Only 21 Maroons managed to surrender within the three days allowed by the Governor. But General Walpole, who felt that the time given was too short, accepted the surrender of some 400 others during January, the last coming in by mid-March.

It was held that the Maroons had broken the agreement by not surrendering by 1 January, and the question of what should as a result be done with them was referred to a joint committee of the Assembly and Council. The committee refused General Walpole's evidence, deciding by a majority of 21 to 13 that the Maroons who had failed to surrender in the time given were not entitled to the benefit of the agreement made on 21 December, and should be transported from the island! Accordingly the entire Trelawny Town tribe – including the six captains who had met Balcarres at St Ann's Bay, as well as Montague and those who had surrendered with him before the war started – were packed onto transports and, with a naval escort, shipped to Halifax in Nova Scotia.

General Walpole was very angry at the government's action and protested as strongly as he could. 'It was through my means alone that the maroons were induced to surrender', he wrote to the Governor, 'from a reliance which they had in my word'. But he was powerless to change what had been done. So bitter was he that he refused a sword of honour which

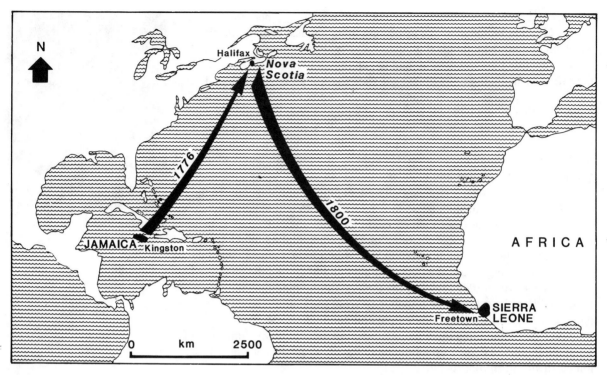

The route followed by the transported Maroons

the Assembly wished to present to him for his services, and later resigned his commission in the army. Balcarres was also voted a sword costing £700; he had earned, in addition, nearly £5000 in extra pay during the period of martial law.

Even in England General Walpole did not let the matter lie. He ran for and won a seat in Parliament and there brought up the subject of the Maroons, strongly condemning the conduct of the Jamaica Assembly in transporting them from the island, but by that time the 'war' attracted little interest and his efforts to have the matter officially investigated failed.

Part of the lands of the transported Maroons was given to those of Accompong. Barracks were built on the site of the old Trelawny Town and regiments of British soldiers garrisoned there until the middle of the nineteenth century. The buildings have long since crumbled into ruins. In Nova Scotia the Maroons suffered acutely from the cold and refused to do much work. Disputes soon arose between the government there and that of Jamaica as to who should pay for the support of the Maroons. Finally, in 1800 they were removed to Sierra Leone in Africa where their descendants are still to be found among the people of Freetown.

So ended the Second Maroon War, and with it the outstanding events in the story of these people. Except for a short time in 1865 (dealt with in a later chapter) when they helped the government to suppress an uprising in St Thomas-in-the-East, they have lived peacefully in their mountain settlements.

Chapter 14

The end of slavery

As we have seen, sugar and the slave trade went hand in hand. Sugar gave the West Indies their importance and without slaves the cultivation of the crop was impossible, such, at least, was the firm belief at the time. So the slave trade flourished, a vital part of Britain's overseas trading activities, a very profitable trade, by means of which labour essential to sugar production was supplied and hundreds of ships and their crews found employment in transporting that labour.

Whether slavery was right, according to Christian principles, was another matter, and although from very early there were people who condemned the system as cruel and unjust, in the main the planter and slave trader were untroubled by such considerations. Among the arguments put forward in defence of the slave trade, when anyone bothered to defend it at all (apart, of course, from the overwhelming argument that without slaves there would be no sugar) was that most of the blacks shipped to the plantations had been slaves in Africa anyway, and that at least in the West Indies they came into contact with civilised living and Christianity.

But as the eighteenth century drew to its close a change began to take place which was eventually to shake the system of slavery to its foundations. For one, certain changes in the industrial and trading life of Britain, too complex to describe in detail here, began to give rise to doubts as to the soundness of supporting the West Indian slave-based economy. But of more importance was the new demand for liberty being voiced in Europe and the wave of humanitarian reform sweeping Britain at the time (the result of a religious revival led by the founder of Methodism John Wesley, and his brother Charles). This wave of reform was to awaken a concern for the welfare of prisoners and other unfortunates, and was to break with force against the structure of slavery itself and help to sweep it away.

As far back as 1671, George Fox, founder of another religious sect known as the Society of Friends, or Quakers as they came to be called, urged all members of his sect in Barbados to treat their slaves well and set them free after a certain period of time. It was also from the Quakers, a few years later, that the first public protest against slavery and the slave trade came when those of Germantown in the American state of Pennsylvania, declared the system to be wrong and prohibited slavery throughout the

George Fox, English religious leader

State. Around this time also men like Richard Baxter, a Nonconformist, and John Locke were writing against slavery. But these people were exceptional: not even all Quakers had given up slavery at this time.

Granville Sharp, Thomas Clarkson and William Wilberforce

Granville Sharp, English abolotionist

The first real steps towards abolition of the trade were taken as a result of the large number of slaves in Britain, brought over from the West Indies and in many cases abandoned by their masters, and through the efforts of a clergyman's son, Granville Sharp. Sharp's interest in the fate of these slaves was awakened one day in the year 1765 when he noticed among the poor patients waiting to be attended by his brother, who was a doctor, a very sick black man named Jonathan Strong. It turned out that David Lisle, a Barbadian lawyer and Strong's master, had beaten him severely (it is said he had battered him on the head with a pistol) and turned him out of doors as of no further use. But for Granville and his brother, Strong would have died. They managed to have him admitted to a London hospital where he eventually recovered, and on his release they found him a job at a chemist's shop. Two years later Lisle met Strong in the street and finding him well and serviceable again claimed him as his property, selling him later for £30 to James Kerr, a Jamaican planter. To make sure that Strong would not escape, they had him kidnapped and lodged in prison until it was possible to get him on a boat bound for Jamaica. As soon as news of what had happened reached Sharp he took up the case and, using all the influence he could, had Strong released. Lisle and Kerr now claimed damages against Sharp for loss of property, but prudently dropped the charge in the end.

Sharp had by now become interested in the plight of these people, and in whether by law slavery was permitted in England. He doubted that it was, and began his efforts to force a court decision on the question. By his help two other slaves, Hylas and Lewis, were rescued. Lewis had actually been tied up, gagged and hurried secretly aboard a ship then ready to sail for Jamaica when an order for his release, secured by Sharp, set him free.

Granville Sharp's work on behalf of the slaves earned him many enemies, but it helped awake public interest in the subject, while the main question that would affect all the blacks in Britain remained unanswered. Still, Sharp worked on, until in June 1772, his opportunity came with the case of a slave named James Somerset. Like Strong, Somerset had been turned adrift in the street because of ill-health by his master Charles Stewart of Virginia. With Sharp's help Somerset recovered, whereupon Stewart claimed him once more as his property. Sharp resisted the claim and the case went to court where it came before Lord Mansfield, at that time Lord Chief Justice. On 22 June he handed down his famous judgement in which he declared that slavery was not 'allowed or approved by the law of England' and therefore Somerset must be set free. This decision, supported by a similar one made by some Scottish judges a few years later, meant that all the slaves in Britain, numbering more than 10 000 at that time, were entitled to freedom whether or not they wished to remain in the service of their masters. It also meant that any slave brought into the country could be regarded as a free man the moment he set foot ashore.

With this case was won the first major battle in the anti-slavery struggle. Sharp had waited nearly ten years for success, more than sixty were to pass before the movement he had set in motion was to end in victory.

The Quakers now formed an anti-slavery committee which was joined by Granville Sharp and two other valuable supporters, James Ramsay and Thomas Clarkson. Ramsay had spent nineteen years in the West Indies as a clergyman where he had seen enough of slavery to be able to write and speak about its evils with authority and conviction. Clarkson as a young man at Cambridge University had written a prize-winning essay on slavery and had become as a result very interested in the subject. So appalled was he at the facts about slavery which he unearthed in preparing his essay that he decided 'it was time some person should see these calamities to their end', and resolved to devote his life to this. Between Ramsay and himself they used all the means they could to arouse public interest in the subject of slavery and make people aware of its evils. Besides gathering a mass of information to support their case, Clarkson also visited the slave-trading ports of Bristol and Liverpool and risked his life collecting objects used in connection with the trade such as shackles, thumb screws and mouth openers. These he later exhibited so that the public could see for itself evidence of the cruelty that was part of the business. Other helpful supporters of the anti-slavery movement were James Stephen, for ten years a practising lawyer in St Kitts, and Zachary Macaulay who had worked on an estate in St Thomas-in-the-Vale.

But, valuable as the work of these men was in getting public sympathy, the slave trade could only be abolished by law, and for this the committee needed the support of Parliament. It was most fortunate, therefore, that William Wilberforce, a man with the qualities and influence necessary to secure this support, should have joined the anti-slavery movement at this stage. Previously he had taken no interest in the subject. An eloquent speaker, rich and witty, he had entered Parliament when only twenty-one years old as a member for Hull (the city where he was born in 1759). His closest friend, William Pitt, later to become Prime Minister entered Parliament at the same time. Used to gay and easy living, Wilberforce gave little thought to the rights or wrongs of slavery until he came under the influence of the religious revival then sweeping the country. Among the people who made an impression on him was John Newton, one time captain of a slaver but now a clergyman and a member of the abolition movement. Clarkson's writing also influenced Wilberforce and helped him to make up his mind to devote his life to the fight against the slave trade and slavery.

The committee, meanwhile, began to organise itself efficiently. Public interest was kept up by pamphlets, talks and lectures on the subject, and the attention of the House of Commons constantly attracted by means of numerous petitions against the slave trade.

Jamaica, it will be noticed, figured prominently in the cases which Granville Sharp used in his early struggle. In 1781 an atrocious incident off

William Wilberforce, English philanthropist

the coast of the island was to help still further to bring the evils of the slave trade forcibly to public view. A Liverpool slaver called the *Zong* sailed from Africa in September of that year with a cargo of 440 slaves, bound for Jamaica. By the end of November 60 had died and most of the others were desperately ill. Knowing that the death at sea of a slave from natural causes meant a loss to the owners, but that the loss was borne by the insurance company in the case of any disposed of for the general benefit of the ship and cargo, Luke Collingwood, the captain, with the help of his crew, threw 132 of the slaves overboard alive! Lack of sufficient drinking water and his wish to save the slaves from a lingering death from thirst was the reason he later gave for his action, but it was clear that this was only an excuse: for one thing, Jamaica had been sighted two days before the slaves were disposed of. The owners were nevertheless successful in their claim against the insurance company. Granville Sharp, however, made good use of the case by having details of the proceedings printed and widely circulated.

So the fight went on to win the support of the British people and the sympathy of Parliament, despite disappointments and defeats in the House of Commons, until 1792 when, with the help of Pitt, Wilberforce got the House to agree the slave trade should be brought to an end after four years.

The West Indian planters and their influential friends in England watched these proceedings with growing anger and alarm, since they saw in them their own ruin. Powerful and well organised, they did not sit idly back, but forcefully opposed the proposals for abolishing the trade, but it was the French Revolution and outbreak of war with Napoleon around this time which gave them a temporary victory. The British government found its attention engaged by more important matters than the slave trade; in addition, the dangerous ideas being preached by the French revolutionists and the events that followed in St Domingue caused people to be rather cautious now about proposals to give the blacks freedom.

It was at this time that Wilberforce proved of greatest value to the anti-slavery campaign. With tireless determination he moved his resolution for the abolition of the trade year after year. In 1803 success seemed certain when the Abolition Bill passed the House of Commons, only to be defeated in the House of Lords. But five years later came victory. The Bill (or Act) was passed by which all trading in African slaves was declared to be, as from 1 January 1808, 'utterly abolished, prohibited and declared to be unlawful'. It should be mentioned to her credit, that Denmark, with her three small West Indian possessions of St Thomas, St Croix and St John (purchased by the United States of America in 1916) had abolished the trade four years before Britain did. Cuba, on the other hand, Jamaica's nearest neighbour, was to continue importing slaves up to 1865.

Emancipation

The Abolition Bill did not bring all trading in slaves to an end. Other nations were free to continue the trade and even in those countries where it had been made illegal a certain amount of slave smuggling went on. Profits were high, and English traders in common with those of other countries, were tempted to turn smuggler. They were soon discouraged, however, by the activity of the British Navy in stopping and searching suspected vessels, and by the passing of severe laws, such as that of 1827, which treated slave-trading as piracy the punishment for which was death.

Most members of the anti-slavery movement regarded abolition of the trade as only a first step; emancipation, that is the freeing of the slaves themselves, was their main interest from the first, although the best way of achieving this was not immediately clear. It was felt by some that the West Indian planter, cut off from the means of importing new slaves, would treat those he had better to preserve them; that he would encourage marriage and family life among them in order to increase his stock; that gradually he would be forced to give them greater rights and freedom which would in time lead to full emancipation. But matters did not work out that way. The abolition of the slave trade had rather the opposite effect on most planters, especially those of the older colonies like Jamaica who had for long been accustomed to making their own laws and now bitterly resented Parliament's action in abolishing by law a trade vital to their interests. Indeed, they tended to treat their slaves more cruelly now in the belief that so doing would discourage any ideas they might get into their heads about freedom. So it soon became evident to the anti-slavery committee that emancipation would have to be forced on the planters.

Wilberforce was still leader of the movement, but age and ill-health made it unlikely that he could continue to carry on the fight in Parliament for much longer. Among the younger members of the House he was to find in Thomas Fowell Buxton an excellent successor. Both men were deeply religious and shared a common hatred of slavery.

In 1823 the Anti-Slavery Society was founded with the Quakers again taking a prominent part, but now among its membership was a number of influential public men, members of both Houses of Parliament and the King's own cousin as president. Knowing the value of keeping public interest in the subject alive, Clarkson resumed his lecture tours throughout the county and Zachary Macaulay took over a publication called the *Anti-Slavery Monthly Reporter*.

Once more the campaign opened in Parliament. Numerous petitions had been sent to the government demanding emancipation, and in May of that year Buxton moved a resolution in the Commons that 'slavery . . . ought to be gradually abolished throughout the British colonies', but by then the government had already decided to do so, by slow stages. Directions were accordingly drawn up and sent to the colonies for the amelioration (that is, the improving) of the conditions under which the slaves worked and lived. These directions required, among other things, that Sunday markets be stopped and the slaves given an extra free day in which to sell their produce; the use of the whip in the field was forbidden, as well as the flogging of women; slaves were also to be allowed religious instruction. A circular was issued at the same time from the Colonial Office to all West Indian governors, calling upon them to see to it that these directions were carried out.

The anger of the members of the Jamaica House of Assembly on receiving these instructions was terrible. They bluntly refused to revise the island's slave laws to include the new amelioration measures, declaring that the laws were complete as they stood, and the slaves contented. Furthermore, they protested most strongly against the interference by the British Parliament in their internal affairs and legislation. Some members were later to go as far as to threaten to transfer their allegiance from Britain to the United States, or to set up an independent republic in the island!

Although the reaction in most of the other islands was similar, not all could take the steps Jamaica did, for there were at this time two types of colony, the older ones such as Jamaica and Barbados with their own elected assemblies, and those known as Crown Colonies such as Trinidad, Guiana and St Lucia, acquired during the recent wars. In the former the assemblies made their own laws, later approved or in unusual circumstances vetoed by the British Parliament; but in the latter, government was conducted mainly direct from London by means of instructions called Orders in Council. In the Crown Colonies, therefore, the amelioration measures were put into effect fairly easily, but the other islands would have nothing to do with them and the British Parliament was most unwilling at this early stage (although it possessed the power) to force their acceptance: deciding rather to be patient, hoping that the example set by the Crown Colonies would in time be followed by all of their own free will – but the hope was in vain. In Jamaica at session after session of the Assembly the Governor brought forward the amelioration proposals, but without success. 'Although there are gentlemen in the Assembly who . . . think that much may and ought to be done in favour of the slaves', the Duke of Manchester reported, 'they are so outnumbered by persons of a very opposite description that I certainly despair'.

The Earl of Belmore who followed the Duke of Manchester as governor, did get the Assembly to alter the island's slave code to some extent, but the changes did not go far enough and were not approved in England, although some progress was made with the passing of a law which permitted slaves to give evidence in courts.

News of these events soon spread to the slaves because their masters, at table, on the streets, in stores and other public places, openly discussed the proceedings of the Assembly and condemned the efforts of Wilberforce, Buxton and the rest of the Anti-Slavery Society, not caring that their words were being overheard and perhaps not clearly understood by their slaves. In fact the slaves soon came to the conclusion that certain benefits conferred on them by Britain were being withheld, and this led to unrest and open revolt, especially in Guiana and Jamaica. The planters were quick to use these disorders to serve their own ends, claiming that the slaves had been perfectly contented until they got it into their heads that the King and Wilberforce had made them free. The slaves, of course, were never contented at any time, as the many revolts dating from the seventeenth century show; nor were they likely to be more contented with slavery now than before. Their restlessness at this time was, in fact, to help hurry the day of freedom, although it was to cost many of them their lives and cause dreadful suffering to many more.

Frequent meetings of slaves in St George's parish some time before Christmas 1823, led to the belief, confirmed by a runaway slave, that plans were being laid for a general revolt, as a result of which those believed to be the leaders were arrested and executed. Still the unrest smouldered. In St Mary, St James, Hanover, even in the neighbourhood of Kingston, trouble broke out and was firmly suppressed by hangings and severe floggings. These events only served to stiffen the resistance of the Assembly to the amelioration measures: in fact the Assembly appealed to Parliament for a contribution towards the cost of suppressing these disturbances since it declared it was the discussions in London that had stirred up the slaves to rebellion!

Sam Sharpe's rebellion

The rebellion, as it happened, was yet to come. Still believing that they had been freed by England but were being held in bondage by their masters, the slaves in the western part of the island organised by one Samuel 'Daddy' Sharpe, a slave and Baptist preacher, went on a sort of general strike during the Christmas week of 1831. This strike soon developed into one of the biggest slave rebellions the island was to experience – and the last of its kind. The great house and sugar works at Kensington Estate in St James,

The destruction in January, 1832, of Roehampton Estate in the parish of St James's

were the first to be set on fire by the slaves; within a matter of hours several other plantations in the neighbourhood were ablaze.

Although St James was the seat of the trouble, minor disturbances broke out far and wide, in St Elizabeth, Manchester, St Thomas-in-the-East and Portland. Kingston and Spanish Town remained undisturbed throughout, but elaborate precautions were taken nevertheless. In addition to the troops stationed in Kingston, a well-armed merchant vessel was anchored off the end of each of the streets and lanes leading to the waterfront, in such a position as to be able to rake them with gunfire if the need arose.

The loss of life was relatively low, but damage done to sugar works and homes was very high and the British government later lent the planters £200 000 to help them restore their properties. The few British troops in the island, under the sound and humane leadership of their commanding officer, Sir Willoughby Cotton, soon brought the revolt under control, but the retaliation by the civil authorities against the slaves who had taken part was prolonged and terrible. A great many were executed and scores brutally flogged. Sharpe himself was hanged for his part in the revolt which, although it had miscarried, helped to hasten the day of freedom he had striven for. The Wesleyan missionary, the Rev. H. Bleby, described Sharpe as the most remarkable and intelligent slave he had ever met. His body is said to have been removed from its original burial place to a grave beneath the pulpit of the Baptist Church in Montego Bay. Today Sam Sharpe is revered as a National Hero and the main square in Montego Bay where he was hanged is now named for him.

The Nonconformist missionaries, especially the Baptists, had never been popular with the planters because of the work they did among the slaves, and now they found themselves being blamed for the disorders. The Baptist preachers William Knibb and Thomas Burchell and the Moravian H. G. Pfeiffer amongst others, were arrested and charged with inciting the slaves to rebellion. They were eventually aquitted. Mr Pfeiffer, on the strength of four slave witnesses, had been arrested and sentenced to be shot. As the jail was full by this time, he was confined in the Mandeville Parish Church. Luckily a militia private who had succeeded in visiting him the day before his execution, by the following morning managed to collect forty witnesses on whose testimony Pfeiffer was in the end set free.

Meanwhile a society called the Colonial Church Union[1] was formed, in theory to protect the Anglican Church but having as its main objects the defence of slavery, the persecution of the Nonconformists and destruction of their places of worship. Salters Hill chapel was burnt down by the St James militia. This was followed by the riotous destruction of Baptist and Wesleyan chapels in St Ann, Trelawny, Hanover and other parishes. The society was only broken by the issuing of a Royal Proclamation declaring it to be illegal, and the strong action of the Governor against those of its members who tried to keep it going.

William Knibb, missionary and anti-slaver

[1] The Rev. George Wilson Bridges is said to have been 'the founder and most energetic leader of the Union'. He was Rector of St Ann from 1823 to 1837 and author of *The Annals of Jamaica*, a history of the island in two volumes, published in 1827. His four daughters were drowned before his eyes through the swamping of a boat in St Ann's Bay.

So the turmoil and violence continued, long after the rebellion had been crushed. In April 1832 a newspaper called *The Watchman* published an article calling upon the 'friends of humanity to give a long pull, and a strong pull, and a pull altogether, until we bring the system [of slavery] down'. The mulatto editor of the paper, Edward Jordon, was arrested and charged with sedition and treason, the punishment of which could at that time have been death. The case actually came to nothing, but he was convicted on another charge, fined and imprisoned. This judgment was later reversed, but by then he had served six months of his sentence.

Jordon, the leader of the mulatto section of the population, was to play an important part in the life of the island for nearly half a century. As in Haiti, these 'free people of colour' as mulattoes like Jordan were also called, had for some time been growing increasingly dissatisfied with their condition. Although free to work for themselves and to own property, they could not vote or hold office. Repeated attempts to get the Assembly to allow them the same rights and privileges as those enjoyed by the white people had, however, been unsuccessful, and in 1820 they formed a secret society through which to carry on the struggle, and elected Jordon, then only 21 years old, as secretary. It was not until 1830 that an Act giving them full civil rights was passed. They were not, as a group, concerned at the beginning with the efforts then being made to have slavery abolished, but after the 1831 rebellion, openly sided with the movement.

Once again the planters and their supporters in England tried to use the rebellion as proof of the dangers of amelioration, and for a time were successful; but their gain was temporary. When all the details were known in England, especially of the persecution of the Nonconformist missionaries, the British people were more convinced than ever that slavery must be abolished.

Again the amelioration proposals were presented to the Assembly only to be again rudely rejected. In fact, the members were more violent than before in their opposition. One of them, a Mr Berry, moved that the Order in Council containing the proposals be carried out of the House into the Square and burnt by the hangman, and he threw his own copy onto the floor as an example to the other members!

The patience of Parliament was now at an end. For nearly ten years all efforts to get the Jamaica legislature to adopt the Orders in Council for the amelioration of the slaves had failed. The time for patient reasoning was past. The West Indian planters had defeated themselves. They had completely lost the sympathy of the British people, not only on moral grounds, but on economic ones as well. The production costs of West Indian sugar at this time were high, owing largely to mismanagement of the estates. Beet sugar from Europe was proving a serious rival, while that made in such places as Mauritius, Brazil and Cuba could be imported more cheaply than could that produced in the British West Indies; but in order to protect her colonies, England had placed a heavy duty on sugar from other sources. As a result the price rose so high that by 1829 many people in England could not afford to use sugar. If slavery could not produce cheap sugar it was no longer necessary and it was therefore in the interests of the British public to have it abolished.

Leading newspapers in Britain now supported the anti-slavery cause, sermons were preached on the subject throughout the country and numerous petitions sent in to Parliament – one with almost a million and a half signatures – demanding emancipation.

Wilberforce was by this time so ill that he could no longer take part in the work of the abolitionists, but his interest never lessened. In July 1833 the Bill to free all slaves was introduced into the House and soon Buxton was in a position to assure Wilberforce that it was certain to go through. It was passed on 29 August 1833, four weeks after Wilberforce had died. He was buried in Westminster Abbey and today his house in Hull is kept as a museum, devoted largely to relics connected with slavery and the slave trade.

Apprenticeship and 'Full Free'

To understand the events of the next few years it is necessary to be clear about the provisions of the Emancipation Act. It provided that as from 1 August 1834, all slave children under six years of age, and any which might be born after that date, were to be free. All other slaves became apprenticed to their former masters, the field-labourers, or predials, for six years (up to 1 August 1840), and the non-predials for four years (up to 1 August 1838), after which time all were to be completely free. While apprenticeship lasted the apprentices had to work for their masters for three-quarters of every week (40½ hours) without wages, the masters on their part being required to continue to provide lodging, clothing, medical attendance and food, or in place of food provision grounds in which the apprentices could grow their own food. For the remaining quarter of the week (13½ hours) the apprentices were free either to work on the provision grounds or hire themselves out for wages. With the money earned in this way the apprentice could, if he saved enough, buy his own freedom with or without his master's consent; or he might be manumitted, that is legally freed, by his master, if the latter wished to do this. A number of Special Magistrates (later known as Stipendiary Magistrates) were appointed by the Colonial Office to supervise the working of the apprenticeship system and see to it that the ex-slaves were not taken advantage of by their former owners. Finally the sum of £20 000 000 voted by Parliament, was to be divided among all the slave owners in the Empire by way of compensation for the loss of their slaves.

To take the last provision first, why, it might be asked, was it thought necessary to compensate the slave owners? Because it was only fair to do so. Until its abolition, slavery in the colonies had been legal according to British law; slaves were valuable property, so if Britain were to force the slave owners to give up their slaves, it was but fair that those owners should be compensated for the loss. Actually, in its early form the Act only provided for a loan to the slave owners of £15 000 000. Of the outright gift of £20 000 000 finally fixed on, £6 149 939 was paid to Jamaican slave owners who, however, owed so much money in the form of mortgages and other debts to creditors in England, that little of that sum came to the island.

Why, it might also be asked, was this intermediate period of apprenticeship thought necessary before complete emancipation, or 'full free' as the blacks called it? It should also be pointed out that in its early form the Act fixed the period at twelve years; as events were to work out, it ended for all types of slaves in four. Actually, in some islands – Antigua and Bermuda for example – apprenticeship was not adopted and all the slaves there were freed as from 1 August 1834; but in Jamaica, as elsewhere, apprenticeship was thought necessary for a number of reasons. First, because the slaves were more backward than in most of the islands and not ready for complete freedom, largely on account of the Assembly's refusal to accept the amelioration measures which would have helped prepare the way and the people for citizenship. Secondly, in islands like Antigua where almost all the land was under cultivation few of the freed slaves could support themselves without working for the sugar planters. But in islands with an abundance of unoccupied land – Dominica, St Lucia, Trinidad, above all Jamaica – there was the fear that with the granting of full and sudden freedom the former slaves would abandon the plantations, settle on lands especially in the interior and set up a kind of jungle society which would be a social danger to the country while causing economic ruin, since production on the plantations would be seriously reduced or cease entirely. While the fear of the formation of a jungle society might have been exaggerated, in Jamaica, at least, if emancipation had come too suddenly there might have been some disorder and perhaps bloodshed.

Although the Jamaica Assembly was the first to enact the Emancipation Law (without doing which none of the colonies would qualify for its share of the compensation money) they did not do so willingly or with good grace. The attitude of the Assembly may be summed up in its frank statement that in giving effect to abolition it did so against its better judgement and only to avoid the still greater danger of opposing it! So, to the very end Jamaicans fought against the forces of change.

The apprenticeship system may not have been perfect, but in view of the spirit in which it was received here, it is not surprising that in Jamaica it worked worst of all. The cooperation of everyone concerned was needed for success, and it was this which was lacking. The planters resented the idea from the beginning and had little or no goodwill either towards the apprentices or special magistrates. And yet the system got off to a good start. The disorders and bloodshed which both the Jamaicans and people of Britain feared might have broken out with freedom did not occur. This was owing largely to the influence of the missionaries. Some of the slaves climbed hill tops on the morning of that first day of August 1834, to watch for the first signs of the dawn of freedom, but the majority welcomed the new day in churches and chapels, giving thanks for their deliverance.

In a dispatch to London dated 13 August, the governor at the time, the Marquis of Sligo, was able to report that the behaviour of the apprentices could not have been better and that all had turned out to work on the plantations except in St Ann. In the eastern part of that parish, which was to be a trouble spot throughout the period, refusals to work were general.

A medallion made to celebrate liberation from slavery

The presence of troops, sent round by sea, frightened the apprentices but did little else. It was the advice of the special magistrates, a few floggings and workhouse sentences which soon restored order and ended the strike. But the system was doomed to failure, and Lord Sligo was forced to write to London shortly afterwards, 'I cannot, after two months trial of the New System, report to you, that it is working at all in a satisfactory manner'.

The *idea* of apprenticeship itself was difficult for the ex-slaves to understand. First they were told that slavery had ended, then that they must work without wages for three-quarters of every week. In fact, if there had been less compulsion in the system it might have succeeded better, but as it stood the apprentice did not have sufficient opportunity to learn the duties and responsibilities of full freedom.

It was to the special magistrates that the difficult and delicate task of instructing the apprentices in the meaning of apprenticeship fell. These special magistrates were composed mainly of men sent out from Britain, but included also a small number of coloured Jamaicans, among whom Richard Hill, the famous patriot, writer and naturalist, deserves special mention. Son of an English merchant and a half East Indian woman, Hill was educated in England and spent two years in St Domingue investigating social conditions there on behalf of the Anti-Slavery Society. Before the end of apprenticeship he had become head of the special magistrates department, a position which he held until his death in 1872. He was offered the lieutenant-governorship of St Lucia, but refused it in order to remain in Jamaica devoting himself to his public duties and valuable natural history work.

The difficulties which the special magistrate had to face in doing his job properly were great. If he took the side of the planter nothing was too good for him, but if he were known or believed to be a friend of the apprentice there was no end to the obstacles which could be put in his way. They were men of all types: some were sincere and intelligent, others not very interested or bright; some were won over by the planters, others went too far to protect the apprentices. Some were failures, but the majority seem to have done their duty with good sense and humanity, many dying from overwork and exposure to all kinds of weather while riding from estate to estate trying cases.

In spite of the efforts of the special magistrates, the problems surrounding the working of the system were never really solved. One of the chief of these was that created by the planter over the daily allotment of work. The law required the apprentice to give $40\frac{1}{2}$ hours labour to his master every week, but did not state how many hours should be given in a day. Both the apprentices and special magistrates tried to get the planters to agree to a nine-hour day, which would enable the apprentices to complete their compulsory labour by midday on Friday and so have a full day and a half for themselves. Most planters, however, insisted on their working an eight-hour day; many also refused to continue the allowances of food to the apprentices, or if they did give food they charged for it, forcing the apprentice to pay in the form of extra labour. Provision grounds, once also a regular allowance during slavery, were now rented to the apprentices, the rent to be paid again by means of extra hours of free work.

Another source of contention was the excessively high valuation which the planters placed on their former slaves in order to make it difficult for them to buy their freedom. In spite of this, almost 1500 bought their freedom in the first two years of apprenticeship. Among the highest sums paid was £111 2s. 3d by Thomas M'Dermot, a predial labourer on Green Castle Estate, St Thomas-in-the-East. Finally, in a determination to grind the very last ounce of work out of their ex-slaves, the planters drove and punished them, in some ways more brutally than they had done while slavery lasted.

It must not be thought that the planters acted in this way because of resentment and spite only, strong as these emotions were. Their main concern from the start was to hold on to as large a labour force as they could in order to keep their estates going; so, many of their actions sprang from the need to tie the apprentices to their service as long as possible.

The planters commonly believed (and to a great extent they were right) that with full freedom the apprentices would almost all quit the estates and settle on inland areas or in the mountains. The answer to this, they felt, was to import white labour from abroad to replace the blacks. The first of these immigrants – 63 Germans from Bremen – arrived as early as 1834. During the apprenticeship period there were other importations of Germans, as well as of Scots and Irish people, but on the whole the experiment was a failure. The majority died, a number left the estates to do domestic work or take jobs in the police force and elsewhere, while a great many left the country on their own or asked to be sent back home. The largest and most important labour immigrations to the West Indies were from India and China. Immigration from India began when the apprenticeship system ended in 1838, and continued until 1917, except for the period between 1839 to 1844. During that time some 33 000 Indians came to Jamaica, while nearly 5000 Chinese arrived between 1860 and 1893. Between 1840 and 1865 efforts were made to attract large-scale migration of Africans in the form of indentured labourers, but the hopes generated by the scheme's early success were not realised. In all some 7500 Africans came under the programme. A few claimed their free return passage after completion of their indenture, but most remained in the island and became a part of the population. To them we owe the *kumina* cult.

In Jamaica there were three well-defined periods in the apprenticeship experiment. The first was marked by confusion and disputes between apprentice and planter. The second period, covering the years 1835 and 1836, saw a definite improvement in relations between the two groups. In the third period improvements slowed down on many estates, on others it was pushed back by the revival of the old contentions, especially over hours of work. William Knibb who admitted an improvement in the middle of 1836, found 'matters . . . daily getting worse' a year later.

It is from the workhouses, as the slave prisons were called, that the most terrible stories of apprenticeship come. These were not under the control of the special magistrates, but of the custos and justices of the parish; in fact, the special magistrate had often to endure the bitter knowledge that the type of punishment he had ordered in no way resembled what was in fact administered in prison.

The discipline of the workhouses was hard and it was usual for prisoners to be worked in chains. The dark cell, solitary confinement, flogging, starvation, the treadmill – these were punishments the apprentice might have to suffer even for minor offences. Of them the most frightful was the treadmill. It is sad to think that it was introduced into Jamaica by Lord Sligo in an effort to help the apprentices! He had always been appalled by flogging, especially that of women, and he intended the treadmill to replace the whip. He could not have known that flogging would have been added to punishment on the treadmill.

Invented by an engineer named Cubitt in 1818 and first used in English prisons, the treadmill consisted of a large hollow wooden cylinder, round the circumference of which was a series of steps. Persons undergoing punishment trod on these steps, their weight causing the cylinder to revolve, compelling them to move quickly from step to step as the cylinder turned. If anyone slipped or fainted while on the mill, they hung by their tied wrists from the overhead handrail while the revolving steps battered them.

It was, in fact, the brutal treatment of apprentices in workhouses and prisons that hastened the end of apprenticeship. Bad reports from the island, in particular from William Knibb, coupled with agitation from other directions led to the appointment, in March 1836, of a select committee of the House of Commons, moved for by Mr Buxton, to inquire into the working of the system, the condition of the apprentices and the laws affecting them. Although not dissatisfied with the system itself, the committee recommended the remedying of certain abuses. In November of that year the newly arrived Governor, Sir Lionel Smith, tried to get the Assembly to pass laws to bring about these remedies – a law, for instance, fixing the apprentice working day at 9 hours; another settling the amount of food allowed to each apprentice – but, as so often before, the Assembly refused to act.

Later that year, the Quaker Joseph Sturge, Thomas Harvey and two friends came out to the West Indies to examine the apprenticeship system for themselves. Their investigations resulted in the publication of three books which were to have a powerful effect on the British public,[1] to revive the anti-slavery feeling and raise the question as to whether, since apprenticeship was working so badly, it should not be abolished; but motions to that effect moved in Parliament were not at first successful.

And so the time drew near for the complete emancipation of the non-predial apprentices. Now the question began to be discussed as to whether estate artisans – carpenters, coopers, smiths and masons – were to be considered as predial workers or not. It was at length officially decided in England that they were non-predials and must therefore be freed on 1 August 1838. It was not possible, however, to run the estates without these men, and as they would probably all go into other employment as soon as they were free, there was little point in continuing to hold the field labourers any longer. Accordingly, resolutions were moved in Parliament that

[1] In particular the *Narrative* of James Williams, describing the barbarous treatment of an apprentice of that name.

Emancipation, 1 August, 1838

predial apprenticeship should end also on 1 August 1838.

In May of that year reports reaching Jamaica showed that some of the West Indian islands, including Barbados, had passed acts of general emancipation and that a number of others intended to do the same. Proprietors in England sent orders to their attorneys in the island ordering them to give general freedom to all their apprentices on 1 August. It was now clear to the Jamaica Assembly that it could hold out no longer, but to the end its members argued and protested 'before God and man' against the interference of Parliament in the affairs of the island.

Freedom itself came to Jamaica amidst peace and joyful thanksgiving.

Chapter 15

The decline of the plantation

In Jamaica, 1 August 1838 brought freedom from slavery to some 311 000 black and coloured people. They were no longer the property, nor the responsibility, of their former masters. How would they spend their freedom? What provisions were made to help them (and, for that matter, their former masters) to fit into the new way of life? What effect was this great social change, this revolution, to have on the life of the island as a whole?

Even before apprenticeship ended it was clear to the government in England that at least one provision had to be made – for the better running of the workhouses and prisons in the West Indies. As we have seen, it was the brutal treatment of apprentices in these prisons which helped bring the apprenticeship period to an abrupt end. But what now could happen to any ex-slave who might be sent to prison gave cause for great concern. The slight protection provided by the law for the apprentice no longer extended to him, but the management of the prisons *still* remained in the hands of the local magistrates. So, in 1838, Parliament hurriedly passed a bill empowering the governors of the West Indian islands to take over the management of the prisons.

If the Emancipation Act could have caused the members of the Jamaica House of Assembly so much anger and resentment, as being an interference with the right to make their own laws, it may be imagined what effect the Prisons Act produced, for it was concerned, after all, with a purely domestic matter. Most of the islands protested against the Act. Jamaica's protest being, as usual, the strongest. The Assembly objected on the grounds that the internal government of the island was its affair, not Parliament's, and refused to conduct any business – even the passing of annual laws to provide for a police force and the collection of taxes – unless it was annulled. The governor, Sir Lionel Smith, did his best to get the members to accept the Act, but in vain, so he dissolved the Assembly; however the newly-elected House, consisting mainly of the same members, took the same stand in the matter.

Parliament, by now, had had enough of the Assembly's obstructions and decided to suspend the island's constitution for five years, during which time the power to make laws would rest with the governor and the council only. This decision was to cause a political crisis in England and to gain the local Assembly a victory. The bill to suspend the constitution, when put to the vote, was carried by a majority of five only. The cabinet then in power, feeling that so narrow a margin was equal almost to a defeat and would weaken its authority in the empire, resigned. This meant that another cabinet would have to be formed, but in the end the prime minister and his government resumed office, largely because the young Queen Victoria did not wish to change the ladies of her household, which by custom she would have had to do if a new political party came into power. A less drastic course was adopted than that of suspending the constitution; the governor and council were given the power (if the assembly continued to refuse to act) to pass revenue laws and revive any annual laws which might expire. Further, Sir Lionel Smith who had by now become very unpopular, was recalled and replaced by Sir Charles Metcalfe, one of the ablest governors the island ever had. With tact and statesmanship, he was successfully to smooth out the difficulties over the Prisons Act and persuade the Assembly to proceed once more to business. Sir Charles (afterwards Lord) Metcalfe, was born in 1785. He came to Jamaica from India after a brilliant career there which ended in his being made Governor-General. From Jamaica he was appointed to Canada where he also became Governor-General. He was popular with all sections of the Jamaican people, as the statue erected to his memory shows.

The Assembly, by now, was no longer really representative of the people it should have been serving, and its conduct of affairs during this period was utterly confused. As a result of absenteeism few of the early white planter families, or their descendants, were still on the island. Their place was taken by the attorneys sent out to manage the estates: men, in general, of a not very good type who now found themselves in positions of power and importance and holding seats in the Assembly.

The membership of the House now also included a number of coloured Jamaicans of whom Edward Jordon was at this period the most outstanding. He was Mayor of Kingston for fourteen years and was to serve as Speaker of the House of Assembly from 1861 to 1864.

The freed slaves

To return to the subject of the newly-freed blacks. Apart from the Prisons Act which was meant to improve the running of West Indian workhouses, no provisions whatever were made either by the British or local government for the future of these people. During slavery they had huts in which to live, land to cultivate and often medical attention since most large estates had their own hospitals. Who, now, would provide these necessities? The black man was free to look after himself or starve. If he wanted a house he must pay rent, if he needed land he must buy it. To do these things he had to work and save, for the freed slave had no money or possessions to speak of. He was at least free, however, free to choose his employer and haggle over wages.

Meanwhile the need of the planter for labour to run his estates was greater than ever and the urge of many of the freed slaves to get away from the scene of their slavery remained strong – opposing desires which could only mean distress for both sides. The solution lay in a policy of give and take, of continuing, for a time at any rate, the old way of life even if the name were changed, but it was a solution not always adopted. Some property owners spitefully turned the blacks away, preferring to experiment with the immigrant labour then coming into the island; others charged high rents for huts and provision grounds which they knew could not be paid; the more practical allowed their ex-slaves to remain on the estates and, while keeping wages as low as possible, employed them in estate work. On the other side, many of the newly freed slaves were backward and undisciplined and went off into the bush to settle, or more often squat on lands owned by the Crown, growing only enough food to supply their few wants. Others stayed on with their former masters, in their cottages and amidst the provision grounds and well-fruited gardens to which they had become attached, trying to make the best of the situation. Relations between employer and labourer, however, remained unsatisfactory, with much bitterness on the one hand over irregularity of work and on the other over high rentals and low wages.

As the Maroon townships show, Negro villages had been set up even before emancipation came; now, freedom gave greater encouragement to such settlement. With the help of the Baptist missionaries, free villages began to be established on a large scale. The first of these, started in 1835 by the Rev. J. M. Phillippo for the freed slaves, was Sligoville (named in honour of the governor) situated in the hills behind Spanish Town. Three years later Knibb, with Joseph Sturge's help, settled seventy families on a 200-hectare site in St Ann and established the village – complete with church and schoolhouse – now known as Sturge Town. The other Baptist missionaries Clarke, Dendy and Burchell, encouraged and assisted the setting up of free villages and, in so doing, helped the process that was to change the emancipated slaves into peasant proprietors or freeholders. Within five years nearly 200 of these villages, including Bethany, Buxton, Clarksonville, Wilberforce, had been established; by 1840 there were about 8000 peasant freeholders and within five years the number had jumped to 19 000. These farmers were almost self-supporting, earning cash for their needs from the sale of the provisions grown on their small allotments.

The decline of sugar

While these free villages were being established, the island's plantation system was crumbling. As already mentioned, the French wars and the collapse of sugar production in St Domingue, had brought a period of great prosperity to the British West Indian sugar planter, but harder times were on the way. The abolition of the slave trade in 1807 pushed up the cost of production, emancipation tended to increase still further the shortage of labour as well as costs, and production itself steadily declined. This was also caused partly by increasing inefficiency in management and cultivation through absenteeism of proprietors, and especially exhaustion of the land by overcropping. It is true that the sugar planter could count at least on a sure market for his product in England where it was protected by the heavy duty placed on sugar from other sources, but with increasing production costs his profits grew steadily less.

Before emancipation the planter did not have to pay wages, but now he had to find cash to meet a regular wage bill, and because of the shortage of workers he had to purchase labour-saving equipment such as ploughs and harrows to replace the large gangs of slaves armed with hoes, and steam engines for running the mills. But most planters were heavily in debt, or – in the case of those who had paid their debts out of the compensation money – short of capital. Most could not so much as pay their labourers. 'Under slavery a man's wealth had been reckoned by the number of slaves he owned. Now it was reckoned in terms of money, and money was even shorter than labour.'[1]

Strenuous efforts were made to hold off the economic ruin which seemed to draw nearer day by day. Banks were formed to meet the need for capital – the Colonial Bank for the West Indies in London, in 1836, and in Jamaica the Planters Bank shortly after – but they were insecure. Immigrants were brought into the island to help meet the need for labour, but, as already shown, with little success.

Agricultural societies were started in most parishes, and various forms of encouragement offered the planter such as grants for the cultivation of indigo, cocoa, divi-divi, silk, cotton, tea. Silk and cotton production gave early promise of success, but failed in the end. The same was true of tobacco growing. Attention even turned once more to the copper mines scattered about the country, but mining operations did not prove financially worthwhile. A drawback to all these development schemes was the very poor state of the roads.

Rice had been grown in Jamaica, in a very small way, as far back as the seventeenth century. With the arrival of East Indians cultivation was revived, until in time rice was to become a daily food for all classes of Jamaicans. Attention was turned as well to the general improvement of livestock, and new breeds of cattle were introduced. The period saw also the replacing of the old packet brigs by steamships of the Royal Mail Company, and the opening of the first section of the Jamaica Railway Company's line, from Kingston to Angels, a short distance beyond Spanish Town.

In spite of these measures, disaster was fast drawing near. In 1846 the blow fell with the passing of a law in England to equalise the tariff on sugar, and, eventually, to abolish all protective duties which favoured the colonies. In a few years Jamaica's sugar, rum, coffee and other exports had no protection against the cheaper products from slave-owning countries

[1] J.H. Parry and P.M. Sherlock, *A Short History of the West Indies* (London, 1956) p. 198.

like Cuba and Brazil. This action resulted from the adoption of a Free Trade policy intended to make England an industrial nation with a lowered cost of living. The policy was successful: it heralded a period which was to witness the rise of Britain in power and wealth, but was also to see the rapid decline of the British West Indies.

Sugar prices began to fall alarmingly. A commercial crisis in Britain the year after the Sugar Equalisation Act was passed, plunged into bankruptcy a number of West India merchants there who had in the past provided credit for the planters; the Jamaica Planters Bank failed, as did the West India Bank with its head offices in Barbados and branches in many islands. Sugar prices fell still further. The planter as a class was ruined, the coffee plantations having collapsed even more rapidly than the sugar estates.

Some plantations were abandoned because they were so heavily in debt; others had to be sold for whatever they would fetch; many were bought by attorneys who cut them up into small lots and sold them to small settlers; a few were kept intact and struggled on. A visitor to the island at this time, the Rev. John King, who came out from Glasgow to inspect the Presbyterian missions, describes how he rode for kilometres in the country parts over fertile ground which used to be cultivated, but was now lying waste. Trees grew out of the walls and roofs of estate buildings and one had 'to seek about the bush' to find the entrances to houses. Everywhere were neglected fields, crumbling buildings, broken fences, silent machinery. Even Kingston shared in the general decay. A large part of the city had been destroyed by fire some years before, but little had been done to repair or rebuild the houses. 'There is not a foot of street pavement to my knowledge in Kingston', wrote another visitor, 'and the streets are almost uniformly from one to three feet [25 cm to 1 metre] lower in the centre than at the sides. This is the result of spring rains which wash down the mountains in torrents and through the streets of the City to the sea, often making such channels in them as to render them impassable'.

The Sugar Equalisation Act caused a crisis in the Assembly which declared that it was now financially impossible to run the government as before, or to continue to pay the cost of East Indian immigration. The disputes which followed between the Assembly and the government in England resulted in the passing of an 'Act for the Better Government of the Island', described later.

To add to the distress came the threat of a rebellion of the black section of the population because of a rumour that the United States of America planned to take over the island and reintroduce slavery. The alarm was quieted only by the issuing of a proclamation by the governor, denying the truth of the rumour. As if these troubles were not enough, droughts, earthquakes and, in 1850, an outbreak of Asiatic cholera all added to the general misery. This deadly disease, which started in Port Royal, aided by the insanitary conditions existing at the time, soon spread to almost every parish. Some 32 000 people died from it, or about one in every thirteen of the population – a high figure. Yet Jamaica was fortunate; the death rate is often fifty per cent. An outbreak of smallpox in 1852, and the reappearance of cholera the following year (this time in milder form than before) took still more lives.

It was during the cholera outbreak of 1850 that Mary Seacole, one of the most famous of Jamaican women, began her career as a nurse. Born in Kingston at her mother's hotel Blundell Hall, East Street (close to the present site of the National Library of Jamaica), she early showed an interest in nursing and helped her mother who was well known for her skill in curing fevers. During the cholera outbreak Mary learnt a good deal about the disease and its treatment from the doctors with whom she worked, and even made up a medicine of her own which she is said to have used with success. In Cuba, one of the many countries to which her love of travel led her, she became known as 'the Yellow Woman from Jamaica with the cholera medicine'.

She went to the Crimea during the war there which started in 1853, and tended sick and wounded soldiers. She soon became known as the Jamaican Florence Nightingale, after the great English nurse and hospital reformer of that name whose fame also started with her work in the Crimea. Mary died in 1881.

What were the effects of these disasters on the recently emancipated people? They were not ruined by the Sugar Equalisation Act in the sense that the planters had been, but their general condition naturally took a serious turn for the worse. With the collapse of the plantations, large numbers of these people who had depended on them for employment found themselves without work. Those who were still needed by the estates that struggled on had to be content with starvation wages. Market prices for peasant-grown produce had fallen, making the often long walk to a market town scarcely worth the effort, while frequent droughts led to crop failure and increased distress. 'If ever there was a time when it was necessary that something should be done by a Government for a people, this is the people, and now is the time', wrote a stipendiary magistrate, Thomas Witter Jackson in a report on his district which was forwarded by the governor to England. But little was done. Time passed, and a grim crisis slowly took shape. Unable to speak with authority for themselves, and lacking the means to bring their sad plight to official notice, these people looked desperately round for someone who would speak and act for them. They found such a person in the mulatto, ex-slave, George William Gordon.

Chapter 16

Political changes

To understand fully the events which follow, it will be valuable at this point to consider in more detail than has been possible so far how the island was governed during the years 1661 to 1860, and to trace the political changes that had taken place.

Owing to the unsettled state of affairs during the first six years of the English occupation, Jamaica was kept under military rule, that is it was governed by court martial (military court). This court sat once a month in Spanish Town, with Colonel D'Oyley presiding to deal with necessary business. It was not until the Spaniards had been finally expelled that a start was made to set up a civil government.

By that time Charles II had been restored to the English throne, and the promises of rights, land and political freedom made to settlers in the island by Oliver Cromwell no longer held; in fact, no one now knew if Jamaica would be kept or handed back to Spain. As it happened, King Charles and his government wished to retain the island and were eager to continue its development, and so they early announced that they intended to make good Cromwell's promises. This policy, which resulted in the setting up of civil government, had as one of its main purposes the development of the island by attracting settlers to it, many of whom were hesitating to go out until they were satisfied as to the form of government under which they would have to live. The other British West Indian colonies already had their own representative governments: it was important that Jamaica should now have the same.

So, in June 1661, D'Oyley received his commission as governor and instructions to release the army, to set up civil courts of justice and to govern with the advice of a council of twelve persons chosen from among the inhabitants. It is said that D'Oyley was by nature unsuited to the new rôle of civil administrator and asked to be relieved of his office. Whether this is so or not, within five months Lord Windsor had been appointed governor in his place. Windsor brought with him the island's seal, a mace and the King's proclamation promising all English subjects in the island the same rights as those enjoyed in England. He was also authorised, on the Council's advice, to call assemblies to make laws which would be in force for two years only, unless approved by the King, and, when necessary, to raise money by taxation.

Windsor was able, therefore, to assure settlers who might be thinking of coming out to the island that they would be governed by the laws of England and such other laws as they themselves might make, as long as these were not contrary or objectionable to English laws. In order to make such laws for themselves there would be an assembly (elected by the settlers) which would share its authority with the Governor and a council (nominated by him) under the supervision of the English Crown. This was the beginning of what is known as representative government.

The first Assembly of the island did not meet, however, until January 1664, and the irritation of its members at the delay in calling it together shows how much Jamaicans of that day valued their form of government. Laws passed since 1662 by the Governor and Council were declared to be invalid since they had not been consented to by 'the people in Assembly'. The Assembly also did all it could to make sure that the control of money matters, the voting, collecting and spending of funds, would rest with it – the elected body – and not with the Council. Although the next Assembly that was called gave up this ambitious financial policy, it passed an act providing that Jamaican freeholders should enjoy all the privileges and freedoms of English subjects, including the right of consent to their own taxation. The purpose behind this was to safeguard against the Crown's imposing what taxes it pleased – a fact which the King and his advisers were quick to see through, and partly on account of which they did not approve the island's laws sent up for confirmation.

For a time commerce occupied the attention of the colonists and politics were set aside, until around 1671 when the Assembly became active again. From then on, frequent sessions were held, and, as the Assembly grew more vigorous so it became more aggressive, claiming for itself privileges equal to those of the House of Commons in England and setting about meanwhile to take away by degrees the privileges of the Council and special powers of the Crown as discharged by the Governor.

For a time the Assembly had its way. The government in England, busy with more weighty matters, apparently took no notice of what was then happening in Jamaica, until 1678 when a change of England's policy towards her colonies made a closer control of the Assembly and a drastic reduction of its power desirable. This could only now be secured by taking away the island's constitution, that is, its form of government.

As told in Chapter 6, the Earl of Carlisle was appointed governor and given the task of introducing the new constitution, which, it was said, was necessary because of the irregular, violent and unwarrantable proceedings of the Assembly. Under the new form of government the Assembly would lose all power of making its own laws, being able only to approve those laws which were drafted by the Governor and Council and confirmed by the King. The Assembly, naturally, rejected the change and, after a two-year resistance led by Samuel Long, won back the old constitution. England gave up her policy (perhaps as it has been said because it was found to be illegal to take away the Jamaica constitution), and from 1680 on the previous system of government was resumed. With this victory the island's first constitutional crisis was safely weathered.

But there were other problems still unsolved. Because of the Assembly's determination to control all money matters and its refusal to vote a regular sum from each year's revenue for the use of the Crown,[1] the whole body of laws of the island which had so far been passed remained unapproved in England, and government was only carried on by the tedious procedure of re-enacting all expiring laws every two years in order to keep them valid. It was not until 1728 that the troublesome question was settled when, in return for a permanent yearly revenue of £8000 (later raised to £10 000) the Jamaica laws were approved by the King. In addition, it was enacted that all such laws and statutes of England as had at any time been received and used as laws in the island should continue to be so for ever.

From then until 1839 there was to be no further interference with the island's constitutional rights from England. This does not mean that all went smoothly in the government. The opposite was rather the case. There was almost constant quarrelling between the two branches of the administration and the governor, mainly over the subject of rights and prerogatives; besides, controversies developed between the government here and that in England which were to come to a head in 1839.

Before going on, it is important when discussing 'representative government' to be clear as to who, at the particular time, was represented, and who did the representing. At the beginning of civil government there were 4205 people in the island, the proportion of white to black being roughly 5 to 1 (a coloured section such as soon developed, had not yet appeared). In ten years the population was 17272 – more than four times as many, and with the blacks now already outnumbering the whites by nearly two thousand. The original intention in settling Jamaica was to make it a white colony with many small landowners and white indentured labourers. But this intention was changed by the exploits of the buccaneers, and the development of the sugar industry which made necessary the importation of great numbers of slaves from Africa. Soon the proportion of whites to blacks altered completely, so that by 1775 this stood at 12 737 to 200 000! In spite of these changes one class of people – the white landowners, sometimes called the *plantocracy* – had all the say in government for nearly 150 years. From this class came most of the members of council and assembly, and it was their interests which were represented. No black could vote or hold office. Nor was colour the only barrier: for a long time Jews, Roman Catholics and Dissenters were to suffer similar political disabilities.

But these conditions could not last indefinitely. One of the factors which helped to bring about a change was the growth in numbers and importance of a class, between that of black and white, called the free people of colour. From the earliest days of settlement many of the white planters lived with slave women without marrying them. The children born of this mixture of the two races were known as mulattoes. They were by law slaves, but it became usual for their white fathers to secure their freedom for them, with the result that in time the number of free coloured grew. By the 1820s they far outnumbered the whites. Many had taken up professions, others gone into business and, despite the laws which were designed to prevent them as a class from owning property, some had acquired considerable wealth.

[1] Barbados had regularly contributed some of its annual revenue to the Crown, burdensome though this proved.

They were engaged in the cultivation of coffee on a large scale, were the most important pimento producers and in 1826 had claimed to own about 50 000 slaves. A high proportion of the militia, on which the island largely depended for defence, consisted of free coloured, and yet these people had few political rights. It was, thanks to the tireless efforts of men like Richard Hill, Alexander Simpson, Edward Jordon and Robert Osborne, that an Act of 1830 was passed which permitted these people to vote at elections and so gave them the first chance to play a part in the political life of the island. Four years before, the vote had been extended to Jews.

Three years later came emancipation, and on 1 August 1838, 311 000 human beings who till then had had no political rights became full citizens. It was the intention of the government in England that their freedom should be complete, and not from bodily slavery only. This was particularly the concern of James Stephen, the Colonial Office official and one of the best friends the West Indian Negro ever had, whose duty it was to draft the Emancipation Act; but he and the Colonial Office had to reckon with the Jamaica Legislature in the matter. Political control in the island through the Assembly still rested with the same small ruling class of whites and coloured. In 1834 and 1836 they passed acts which, by raising the requirements a man must have before he might vote, were designed to prevent the blacks from voting, when they had been freed. Both acts, through Stephen's influence, were later disallowed in England, but the Jamaica ruling class found other ways of restricting the number of people who could vote, while seeing to it that the requirements[1] for membership in the Assembly were so high that only the rich propertied class could meet them.

As we have seen, the Jamaica Assembly contended with the Imperial Parliament over every step on the road to freedom – over the abolition of the slave trade, amelioration measures, apprenticeship and emancipation itself – but a crisis between the two (described in Chapter 15) did not come until 1839 with the passing by Parliament of the West Indies Prisons Act. This ended in victory for the Jamaicans, but not so that struggle which developed as a result of the Sugar Equalisation Act of 1846.

In a bold gamble to win back the protective duties which were to be abolished in 1854, the Assembly decided on measures which it must have known were bound to create a crisis in the island's government. It began by calling for retrenchment, that is, the cutting down of expenditure beginning with the salaries of high-paid government officials, which, it declared, the island's finances would no longer be able to meet. The Governor and Council would not approve this measure and a deadlock between the two branches of the government developed. Bill after bill embodying the Retrenchment scheme was passed session after session by the Assembly, only to be rejected by the Council. Other measures introduced by the Assembly included one designed to end East Indian immigration, again on the ground that the island could not afford the expense.

So the crisis dragged on until 1852 when the Imperial Parliament once more refused to restore protective duties and the Jamaica Assembly refused

[1] These were, an income of £180 a year from land, or real property worth £1800, or both real and personal property worth £3000.

to do any business. The annual laws expired by which the import and rum duties were levied, and as there was no government to renew them the island became as it were a free port. As a result of this £130 000 is said to have been lost in revenue. Every effort made by Sir Charles Grey, the then governor, to bring the two branches of the government again into friendly relations failed. The dispute had now taken on a personal character and the Governor was being accused of influencing and supporting the Council. It was perhaps fortunate that his term of office expired at this time, and Sir Henry Barkly[1] was appointed in his stead. Declaring that what Jamaica needed 'at the present stage of her political progress was a strong Executive Administration', he managed to secure the adoption of an act for the better government of the island, in return for a guaranteed loan from England to finance the running of the country. Under the new constitution individual members of the Assembly lost the right to propose expenditures of money, a new Privy Council was formed consisting of sixteen members, and the island's first Executive Committee appointed to frame the annual estimates and improve relations between the Governor and Assembly. The first members of this Committee were Edward Jordon, Henry Westmoreland and Bryan Edwards.[2] Under this constitution executive government was to be conducted on the final responsibility of the Governor who was, in turn, responsible to the Crown.

Such then, in brief, is the story of the political changes that took place in the island in the two centuries since the setting up of civil government. The new constitution introduced during Barkly's administration did not, as it happened, prove a success, and far more sweeping constitutional changes were at hand. The year 1860 ushered in one of the unhappiest periods in Jamaica's history. World conditions and various local difficulties were to present the legislators and the executive council with problems which, for one reason or another, they lacked the ability to solve. Meanwhile, as shown in the previous chapter, events moved steadily towards a tragedy – the tragedy of the Morant Bay Rebellion.

[1] An ex-sugar planter of British Guiana, Sir Henry had been sent there to settle a similar retrenchment question, which he had managed successfully. He was therefore welcomed heartily to the island by the 'retrenchment party' here. He and his lady were greeted with a sumptuous entertainment and a ball held in the House of Assembly.

[2] He was a nephew of Bryan Edwards, the historian of the West Indies. He practised for some years as a barrister, was knighted and in 1855 succeeded Sir Joshua Rowe as Chief Justice of Jamaica. He died in 1876 and is buried in the churchyard of St Thomas-in-the-Vale.

Chapter 17

The Morant Bay Rebellion

War down a Monkland!
War down a Morant Bay!
War oh! Heavy war oh!
          Folk Song.

A number of factors which were to lead to the Morant Bay Rebellion have been dealt with in the last two chapters. There are others to be considered, among them the person and activities of George William Gordon, around which the episode largely centres.

George William Gordon

Gordon was born about the year 1820, the illegitimate son of a slave woman and her white master. His father, Joseph Gordon, had come out to the island as attorney for a number of absentee-owned sugar estates and later bought several properties himself, among them Cherry Garden, St Andrew, at the foot of the hills north of Kingston, where George William was born. Joseph became in time a member of the House of Assembly and Custos of St Andrew.

With little help from his father, young Gordon taught himself to read, write and keep accounts, and, when he was ten years old, was allowed to go and live with his godfather, James Daly of Black River. Quick and keen-minded, within a year he was working in Daly's business and proving a valuable helper.

Gordon was about eighteen the year slavery ended, an intelligent, handsome, popular young man with a natural gift for public speaking and a keen interest in politics and religion – interests which were to remain with him throughout his life. He had a deep, if unsettled, concern with religion. Brought up as an Anglican, he never completely broke away from the church, although he joined the Presbyterians, and later the Baptists. None of these sects seemed to satisfy him entirely, and he early began to make plans of forming a church of his own.

George William Gordon

He opened a store in Kingston in 1836 and set up as a produce dealer. Richard Hill who met him in that year later said, 'He impressed me then, though young-looking, with the air of a man of ready business habits', as, indeed, he must have been to have achieved the rapid and striking success he did. In 1842 he was able to send his twin sisters to England and France to be educated at his expense, and later on, an elder sister as well. By then he could boast that although he had begun with 'nothing but his energy and business habits as his stock in trade' already he was worth £10 000. Three years later he married Lucy Shannon, the white daughter of an Irish editor.

While Gordon's affairs prospered, those of his father declined. The latter had lost a number of his estates and others were in danger of being taken for debt. It was at this point that he came to his coloured son for help, although he had had no dealings with him since he was a small boy. He had in the meantime married a white woman and raised a legitimate family.

Gordon nevertheless took over his father's tangled affairs, straightened them out as best he could, paid off the debts on Cherry Garden and gave it back to his father and helped support him and his family who never received their brown half-brother in the house, and did not recognise his relationship to them in any way. Yet, we are told, he always spoke respectfully of his father and kindly of Mrs Gordon. But he never forgot his own mother. On one occasion while walking over Cherry Garden with the Rev. King of the Scots Kirk, he pointed to a grass-covered mound of earth among the trees and said, with sudden tears in his eyes, 'My mother is buried there; she was a Negro and a slave, but she was a kind mother to me, and I loved her dearly'.

Some years later when Joseph and his legitimate family decided to live in England, it was Gordon who paid most of their travelling expenses, taking over Cherry Garden for his own use. It is not surprising that he has been described as 'a man of princely generosity and of unbounded benevolence'.

In spite of his many good points, however, he was also excitable and almost irresponsibly reckless at times. Even his business did not prosper always. He lost heavily in dealings in coffee, invested wildly in real estate and his creditors, at his death, lost a good deal of money on their mortgages.

His political career started in the 1850s with his election to the House of Assembly. He ran as a member of what was then known as the 'town party' led by Jordon. This group was concerned mainly with supporting the interests of the coloured middle class of which they were members, but Gordon's interest lay from the start with the newly emancipated poverty-stricken black peasants. Economic conditions were not so bad when Gordon entered politics as they later became, and the other politicians who did not share his views could afford, at first, to treat them lightly, feeling no doubt that he could not really harm their interests.

He was elected to the Kingston Common Council and on more than one occasion acted as Mayor for Edward Jordon. He was also appointed a Justice of the Peace, at intervals, in seven parishes. His business activities were around this time at their height. He bought and leased several properties, mainly in St Thomas-in-the-East, including Rhine estate. This brought him into close touch with the problems of the peasant farmers. He helped them by cutting up idle land and selling small freeholds, at a period when most proprietors were unwilling to sell their land in this way. He became for a time the owner of the *Watchman* newspaper, and was one of the founders of the Jamaica Mutual Life Assurance Society.

Religion continued to be one of his main interests and he carried out his plan for starting an independent Baptist church. He built a chapel in Kingston, often preached in it, helped to set up chapels in the country parts and, although he did not take the title of *Reverend*, selected and ordained deacons, among them one Paul Bogle of Stony Gut, St Thomas. Altogether, Gordon was an unusual character to whom the lot of champion of the black peasant should fall, but that was the rôle he was to play when in 1862 Edward John Eyre was sent to Jamaica to act for the governor, Captain Charles Darling, during the latter's leave of absence in England. Darling was eventually promoted to Australia, and Eyre, after acting for two years, was made governor in his stead.

Paul Bogle

Edward John Eyre

Eyre's appointment was to prove a disaster for the island, although there was nothing in his previous career to suggest that this would have been so. He had gone out to Australia as a young man and there won fame as an explorer, especially of the southern part of the country, where a lake, among other places, was named after him. He was appointed Protector of Aborigines in Australia and was for a time Lieutenant-Governor of New Zealand. He was next sent to the West Indies as Protector of East Indian

Edward John Eyre, British explorer and Governor of Jamaica

immigrant labourers in Trinidad, and later acted as Lieutenant-Governor of the Leeward Islands, visiting St Vincent, Antigua and Dominica.

Varied as his colonial service had been, he lacked the experience and balance necessary for so important a post as that of Governor of Jamaica. Besides, he had certain failings which were bound to lead to trouble and to a clash with Gordon. He was excessively stubborn and, once he had decided upon it, would never give up an idea or plan no matter how wrong it might prove to be. As an example of this, he supported a scheme which had been started before his arrival in the island, to run a tramway down the main road from Spanish Town to Porus. To the small producers, the tramway would have all but closed the only road by which they could bring their goods to market; it was also illegal in some respects, yet Eyre still fought for it. In the end the lines were torn up and the scheme abandoned.

Eyre was ardently attached to the Anglican church, and like many churchmen of his day he had a hatred of Dissenters, especially of Baptists difficult to imagine today. He associated only with the white ruling class to whose interests he was sympathetic. He was incapable of mixing with and understanding the black population, nor did he understand the multi-racial future that was the only possible one for Jamaica.

Gordon, angered by what he termed the governor's 'committal of illegal acts and the continual infringement of the rights of the people', was especially irritated by the manner in which Eyre had appointed an Acting Colonial Engineer and Architect to replace the previous holder of the post who had been involved in the tramway affair. In the Assembly on 21 January, 1864, Gordon launched a scathing attack on the governor, in which he described him as an animal voracious for cruelty and power. He declared, 'If we are to be governed by such a Governor much longer, the people will have to fly to arms and become self-governing.'

Strong words, perhaps even intemperate in the circumstances, but such statements were not uncommon in parliaments and assemblies where members enjoyed the privilege of speaking more freely than elsewhere. In public, Gordon spoke in milder terms and urged the people to use peaceful means to have their wrongs remedied.

Eyre early succeeded in making himself disliked by most sections of the community and his appointment as governor came as a surprise to all, including himself. To Gordon it was a sad blow for he saw in Eyre a tyrant and an enemy – and with good reason. Eyre had removed him from his post as a member of the St Thomas Vestry[1] and as a justice of the peace for the parish because he had dared to call his attention to certain matters which needed correcting. These included the hardships which people awaiting trial had to bear, the lack of medical aid for the sick and of help for the poor. He had also complained about the filthy condition of the prison and reported that he had found there a man dying in the latrine without any attention being given him. The man had applied for alms to the Rector, the Rev. Stephen Cooke, who had sent him down to the lock-up, there being nowhere else for him to go.

The unpleasant facts which Gordon had brought to light did not do much credit to the local magistrates or the Anglican Church, at least in the person of the local Rector. Although it strengthened Gordon's political following, it earned him many enemies. In 1863 he won election as a member of the Assembly for St Thomas and was also elected once more to the Vestry as the People's Churchwarden, the law being at that time that the Established Church should have a member on the Vestry apart from the local clergyman. But his enemies had not forgiven him: the Reverend Cooke applied to the court to have his election made invalid since as a Baptist he had cut himself off from the Established Church. Gordon appealed against his removal, but the Custos of the parish, the German Baron Von Ketelhodt, one of Eyre's firm supporters, took the law into his own hands in the meantime and had him forcibly carried out of the Vestry room by policemen. It was later declared that Gordon's removal from the magistracy, and the transfer from the parish of the Stipendiary Magistrate Thomas Witter Jackson,[2] one of the few whom the people trusted, strengthened the feeling of hopelessness of ever getting justice under Eyre's administration, and helped to provoke the rebellion.

The road to rebellion

Conditions in the island had reached a very bad state by the beginning of 1865. There were the old problems, such as the difficulty the small planter

[1] Later known as the Parochial Board, and now the Parish Council.

[2] His notebook, covering the period April 1863 to January 1865 is in the Jamaica Archives. It contains records of cases and copies of official letters received and written by him. The entries show clearly the nature of the abuses against which Gordon had protested so long.

had in getting land to cultivate; there was unemployment, low wages (the rates for men were from 9 pence to 1 shilling a day), irregularity in their payment and heavy taxation. In addition a series of droughts had ruined most of the provision crops; while the price of imported food, especially of salt fish and grain on which the peasantry relied, had risen steeply because of the civil war then raging in the United States.

In February Dr Edward Underhill, Secretary of the Baptist Missionary Society of Great Britain, wrote a letter to the Colonial Office, drawing attention to these conditions. His sound and moderate description was based to some extent on first-hand knowledge, for he had spent time in Jamaica and had since kept in close touch with developments. The letter was referred to Eyre who gave it wide publicity in order to contradict its charges. This led to the calling of protest meetings in various parts of the island, later known as 'Underhill Meetings'. Gordon himself presided over a huge gathering in Kingston in May at which he called on the people to cooperate in order to make their grievances known.

Meanwhile a number of peasants in St Ann had drawn up a petition to Queen Victoria which they sent to Eyre, complaining of their poverty, made worse, they said, by the drought and lack of employment. They also asked for some Crown Land to cultivate. Eyre forwarded the petition, together with his own unsympathetic comments, to the Colonial Office and received in answer the famous 'Queen's Letter', as this document has come to be known to Jamaica history. Briefly, it stated that the petition had been laid before the Queen who recommended to the labouring classes hard work as the solution to their difficulties, pointing out that it was from their own efforts and wisdom that they must look for an improvement in their conditions.

This was a victory for Eyre. He had fifty thousand copies of the letter printed in poster form and distributed throughout the island. To the peasantry the letter came as a cruel blow. It made many feel that their last hope had died, that 'Missis Queen' herself who set them free had now deserted them: some feared, in fact, that it meant that slavery was to be reintroduced. Most people realised that the Queen would not have permitted a letter of that kind to be written except on the advice of Eyre and others of his way of thinking, as was indeed the case. She is 'too noble-hearted to say anything unkind even to her most humble subjects', Gordon declared, as he urged the people to continue to bring their grievances forward since in time the truth must be known.

But throughout the country anger grew. Anger against the Governor and his advisers, against the magistrates and the planters who helped to keep the people off the land they wanted so badly. And with this anger grew a spirit of unrest, especially in St Thomas where it centred around Paul Bogle of Stony Gut, the man whom Gordon had made a deacon. Uneducated and in many ways ignorant, Bogle was nevertheless an able, energetic person with the masterful character of an African chief combined with the firm belief that he was meant by God to bring justice to the people. He had a good deal of influence and authority in his locality and had raised enough money to build a large native Baptist church. He admired Gordon, supported his politics and secured votes for him at election time. Paul

Bogle's two main helpers were his brother, Moses, and a preacher named James Maclaren. Having lost all faith in the local courts, Bogle and his group are said to have gone so far as to set up their own court system and appoint justices and constables. Gordon probably knew of these activities and may or may not have encouraged them, but there is no reason to believe that he approved the violence and bloodshed which followed. Always he urged the peaceful course: 'We shall have to go before Parliament with a strong petition', he wrote his overseer on Rhine estate around this time. In August Gordon presided over an open air meeting in Morant Bay at which a deputation, including Paul Bogle and Maclaren, was appointed to wait on the Governor and lay its complaints before him. They walked all the way to Spanish Town . . . but Eyre refused to see them. With bitterness in their hearts they tramped the 80 kilometres back to Stony Gut – and to rebellion.

Bogle held secret meetings in the hills and started to drill his men. He paid a night visit to the Maroon village of Hayfield near Bath, declaring on his return that the Maroons had agreed to help him in a quarrel he was expecting to have with the *buckra*. 'The Maroons is our back', he said. Gordon, meanwhile, lay ill in Kingston, still working on the idea of sending a deputation to England.

The rebellion at Morant Bay

Trouble started on 7 October. It was a market day and Morant Bay was crowded with country people. It was also a court day, and the magistrates were sitting when Bogle marched into the town at the head of some 200 men armed with sticks, cutlasses and a few guns, and led by a drum and fife band. He said he had come to watch the trial of one of his followers. An assault case was tried first and the defendant found guilty. Proceedings were interrupted by a young man who shouted to the defendant that he should pay the fine but not the costs. The police tried to arrest the youth for disturbing the court, but he managed to fight his way outside where he was rescued by Bogle's followers and carried safely away. The case in which Bogle had said he was interested was tried next without any further demonstration.

Later, back in Stony Gut, Bogle learnt that warrants had been issued for the arrest of himself and twenty-seven of his men for rioting, resisting and assaulting the police. Three days later a small party of police arrived at Stony Gut. They tried to hold Bogle, but his cries brought a mob of 250 people to his rescue. The police were easily overcome, tied up and threatened with death unless they swore to stop serving 'the *buckra*'. As soon as they were released they hurried back to Morant Bay and reported what happened to the Custos who sent a message at once to the Governor asking for military aid. A meeting of the Vestry was due to be held on the following day and word had reached Von Ketelhodt that the people of Stony Gut intended to come down in force to present their grievances to him. As an added precaution he called out the Bath Volunteers to reinforce those of Morant Bay, in case of trouble.

Around midday on Wednesday the 11th, Bogle and his men started for the town, being joined on the way by more followers from the neighbouring districts. On arriving at Church Corner they raided the police station and took some old muskets with fixed bayonets which they found there. At about 2.30 in the afternoon, amidst a terrible uproar and the sound of horns, conch shells, fifes and drums, Bogle and his followers poured into the square before the court house. The uproar brought the Custos and other Vestrymen out on the porch of the building. The Custos shouted to the mob to keep back and asked them what they wanted, but all was confusion. 'Peace!' he cried. 'War! War!' came the answer.

As the threatening crowd approached, the magistrates urged the Custos to read the Riot Act. Someone threw a soda-water bottle at the Volunteer Captain and cut his head open; the order was given and the Volunteers who had been drawn up outside the court house opened fire. Seven of the rioters fell dead, but the mob rushed the small company of Volunteers before they could reload, killing and wounding a number of them as the rest retreated in disorder. The bugler who was guarding a bag containing the ammunition was harpooned with a fish spear and the bag snatched away. The court house and neighbouring buildings were attacked and later set on fire and some fifteen of the people who had retreated to them for safety – including the Custos – were murdered as they ran from the flames.

Morant Bay was overrun by the rioters; violence and looting flared, the jail was broken open and the prisoners set free. Back at Stony Gut Bogle held a prayer meeting to return thanks to God for his success so far, then settled down to shape future plans. 'It is now time for us to help ourselves', he declared. 'War is at us; black-skin war is at hand . . .' Soon the disorder spread to other parts of the parish as plantations were plundered and some of the white proprietors butchered.

Martial law was declared throughout the County of Surrey, except in Kingston, and prompt action taken to deal with the situation. The warships *Wolverine* and *Onyx* were dispatched as soon as possible to Morant Bay, and troops sent from Kingston and from the hill station at Newcastle. The latter marched through the Arntully Gap and down the Blue Mountain Valley. The Maroons, whom Bogle had expected to help him, joined the forces of the government. The troops met no organised resistance; bands of rebels were headed off in several directions and in a short time either defeated or scattered. Monklands coffee estate was the farthest point north-west reached by the rioters, and, in the other direction, Elmwood, north of Manchioneal.

'All this has come of Mr Gordon's agitation', the Governor declared at once to Edward Jordon the then Island Secretary. But he did not take action against Gordon until his return from a tour of the troubled area where, he later reported in a despatch to the Colonial Office, he found everywhere the most unmistakable evidence that Gordon 'had not only been mixed up with the matter, but was himself through his misrepresentations and seditious language addressed to the ignorant black people, the chief cause and origin of the whole rebellion'. Egged on by the Custos of

Kingston, Dr Louis Quier Bowerbank, he issued a warrant for Gordon's arrest. Bowerbank seems to have been panic-stricken by events. He had had Gordon's office searched and there found an old map of Kingston with certain street corners marked which, he felt sure, indicated locations where rioting or the firing of buildings were to take place. He went to the officer commanding the troops, General O'Connor (the Governor was at Morant Bay at the time) and told him of his discovery and belief that the white people of Kingston were all to be murdered on Sunday the 15th. 'To show my contempt of the proceedings', said the General later, 'I went to church'.

Where Bowerbank failed with General O'Connor, he succeeded with Eyre. When Gordon heard of the warrant he went to Headquarters House in Duke Street to give himself up to the governor. He asked to be allowed to say goodbye to his wife and a short stop was made for the purpose before he was carried, a prisoner, on board the *Wolverine*. Mr Westmorland, a member of the Executive Council who went on board with the Governor, advised him to have Gordon tried by civil law in Kingston, but Eyre had already made up his mind to take him to St Thomas for trial where martial law was in force and where he was certain to be convicted.

At Morant Bay Eyre handed Gordon over to Captain Ramsay, the Provost Marshal, with instructions to try him for treason and sedition and for being associated with people in the rebellion. Ramsay had set up a reign of terror in Morant Bay where prisoners arrested in connection with the uprising were being hanged or brutally flogged on the flimsiest evidence and for the slightest reasons. A man named Samuel Clarke was arrested in Kingston, tried and hanged in Morant Bay only because he had said at an 'Underhill Meeting' in July that the 'Queen's Letter' was a lie and that Eyre ought to be recalled; another, while being severely beaten, turned his head and glared in anger at Captain Ramsay who immediately ordered him to be taken out and hanged! A veteran of the Crimean War who had survived the Charge of the Light Brigade, Ramsay was probably of unsound mind. He later committed suicide.

Gordon was tried on Saturday, 21 October – a hurried trial at which he was given little chance to defend himself. He was found guilty and sentenced to be hanged. The date was fixed for Monday, but he was not told of this nor the actual time until one hour before the sentence was to be carried out. He asked to be allowed to see his friend, Mr Parnther the Wesleyan minister at Morant Bay, but was refused. He was permitted, however, to write to his wife.

'All I ever did was to recommend the people who complained to seek redress in a legitimate way', he wrote. 'I did not expect that, not being a rebel, I should have been tried and disposed of in this way. . . .'

Before the hour had quite passed he was taken out and hanged, with eighteen others, on a boom rigged up outside the ruined court house, the bodies being later thrown into a trench at the back of the building. That same day Paul Bogle was caught by Maroons as he came out of a canepiece near Stony Gut. He chatted calmly as he walked with them down to the Bay. He denied that Gordon had ever told him to kill the white people. His trial by court martial was short. He was convicted and hanged from the arch of the burnt-out court house.

Within three days of the news of the rebellion's reaching Kingston it was checked; within a week it had been fairly crushed; but martial law was continued for long after and the retaliation against the peasantry carried out with extreme brutality. Over 430 men and women were either shot down or executed by sentence of courts martial, some 600, including women, flogged, and more than 1000 houses and cottages destroyed. Apart from the people murdered by Bogle's crowd at Morant Bay the day the uprising started, and a few others killed on outlying estates such as Amity Hall, no soldier, sailor or special constable received any injury during the 'war'.

The Morant Bay trouble started as a local rising against the magistracy and only later, if ever, developed into a revolt against British rule when the cry of colour for colour went up, and the vague idea got round that if the white people were killed off the island would belong to the blacks. The prompt action taken at the start by the Governor quickly hemmed in the rising and checked the possibility of its spreading to other parts of the island. But Eyre and the ruling planter class saw the event in a different light. On 7 November he called the Assembly together. 'A mighty danger threatens the land', he said in his opening address. He described the recent rebellion and compared the butchery committed by the rebels with that of the Indian Mutiny.[1] He said there was a plan to make Jamaica a second Haiti ruled by blacks who would expel the white people and destroy their property, and called upon the members of the Assembly to save their country from this danger by surrendering the present constitution and so open the way for the setting up of a 'strong government'.

There was a small group of members, led by Samuel Constantine Burke, who opposed the surrender of the constitution to the end. Burke, on one occasion, rose up in the House and said that the Assembly must have gone mad! But Eyre had successfully played upon the fears of the others, and the island's two hundred year-old constitution was given up in exchange for the Crown Colony form of government.

In January of the following year, as a result of a growing demand in England for the whole truth concerning the Morant Bay trouble, a Royal Commission was sent out to inquire into the origin and suppression of the outbreak. An immense amount of evidence was collected and the whole case thoroughly examined. Briefly, the Commission found that the disturbance originated in a planned resistance to lawful authority, gave Eyre credit for his prompt early action, but held him responsible for the continuance of excessive severity, and for the method of Gordon's trial and execution. Eyre had been suspended during these investigations and, so damaging was the Commission's report, he was recalled to England and dismissed from the service.

In August Sir John Peter Grant arrived as governor.

[1] A revolt of the native troops in the Bengal Army, against the British, which took place in 1857. The horrors of this mutiny would have been fresh in the minds of people like Eyre and his advisers, and might have played a part in their handling of the Morant Bay uprising.

Chapter 18

The new Jamaica takes shape

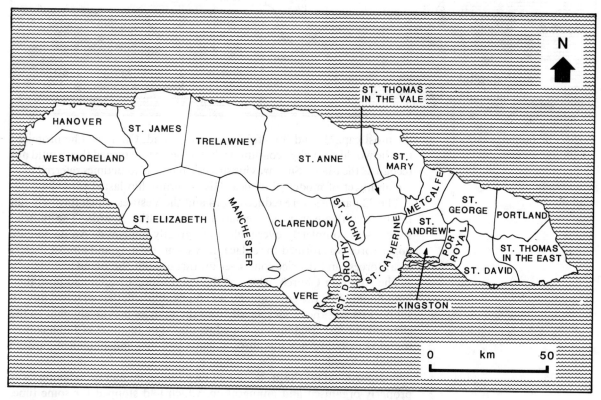

The year 1865 was a turning point in the island's history. It marked the end of what has been called 'the dark age' which had begun in 1838, and it is a good point from which to view the new Jamaica taking shape.

Largely because of the wide powers which they had under the Crown Colony system, the governors of this period were able to push through many reforms and improvements of far-reaching importance. This was particularly true of the first of these governors, Sir John Peter Grant, one of

Parishes of Jamaica in 1844
(first half of nineteenth century)

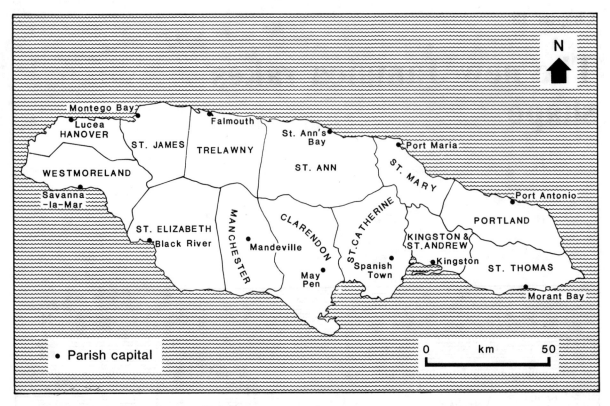

Parishes of Jamaica today

the most capable and forceful Jamaica ever had. On arrival he promised that he would so change conditions that if the dead returned they would not recognise the island. Such was his success that he is sometimes referred to as the architect of modern Jamaica. His governorship lasted till 1874.

The 22 parishes were reduced to 14 and the Vestries which formerly ran local (parish) government, replaced by Parochial Boards. The judicial system was completely overhauled and greatly improved. An up-to-date police force was formed to replace the various existing and almost useless local forces, and district courts set up throughout the island.

The Anglican Church, which as the Established Church had until then been financed by the government, was disestablished; that is, it had now to support itself – the money saved from the salaries previously paid to the clergymen being used instead for education. The Institute of Jamaica was founded to encourage literature, science and art, and botanical gardens were developed.

A department for the protection of East Indian immigrant labourers was properly organised and immigration, which had stopped for some time, resumed. A government savings bank with branches in the parishes was set up, as well as an island medical department, a government medical service and a public works department. Cable communication with Europe was established and transport greatly improved by building roads and railways and starting a street car service in Kingston. The cars, which ran on steel rails, were drawn by mules. The passing of legislation enabling aliens to own land here on the same terms as British subjects did, paved the way for the development, by Americans, of the banana export trade, and, by Cubans, of the tobacco industry, to the country's benefit.

In 1872 the capital was transferred for good from Spanish Town to Kingston, and many improvements to the public amenities of the latter carried out, notably the water supply, the fire brigade, the gas works, the Victoria Market and Pier, and the Parade Gardens which, until 1870, was a dusty open square.

It is in the development of health and social services and education that we see striking evidence of the growth of the new Jamaica. During slavery large estates kept their own hospitals and doctors for the care of sick slaves. The treatment might have been rough and ready, but at least there was some provision. This ended with emancipation, and no real alternative arrangements were made for the large freed population. The case, brought to public notice by Gordon, of the sick pauper who was sent to the Morant Bay lock-up because there was nowhere else for him to go, gives an idea of the conditions that existed at the time, conditions which the events of 1865 were to help bring to an end. It is worth noting that today Morant Bay has one of the biggest hospitals in the island.

It is, of course, a fact that up to the first half of the nineteenth century, people the world over knew on the whole next to nothing about the causes of diseases and, therefore, thought little of the importance of sanitation or preventive medicine. Even in Kingston, at its eighteenth-century peak of wealth and importance, dunghills abounded and from these the ruts in the streets were filled up after heavy rains. Sewage from the houses was carried by slaves in open tubs to the waterfront and simply dumped into the sea. All around, the mosquito-breeding swamps lay undrained, with the result that epidemics were a regular part of life.

'. . . death stalks forth in almost every breeze.
Who dies this morn, ere night is in the grave'.

wrote a sailor-poet aboard his ship at anchor in Kingston Harbour. Typhoid and dysentery, cholera and smallpox, malaria and yellow fever killed off thousands. Either one built up a resistance to the disease or died of it. Today these ailments have been all but banished by sanitation and preventive medicine.

About the middle of the nineteenth century public health in England became by law the concern of the government with remarkable results. By insisting on the improvement of water supplies and enforcing precautions against bad food and epidemics, the Sanitary Commission of 1869 added years to the life of the people. Similar results were achieved in Jamaica by the measures started during Grant's governorship – including free medical services, improved water supplies and better quarantine arrangements – measures which laid the groundwork of the present public health services.

Education

The growth of education followed a broadly similar course. During the early period of settlement education was almost entirely neglected. Planters' children got what little learning they did in their home; later it became the custom to send them to schools and colleges in England, and in a few cases in America. In the eighteenth century a number of bequests were made by wealthy residents for the education of the poor of their parish, meaning as a rule poor white or slightly coloured children. Often the money left was too small to be very useful and some bequests were stolen or lost from neglect. Since about ten was the usual number of pupils per school, the public as a whole could have benefited but little from them.

Among the schools started in this way the following are still in existence: Alley School and Manchester High School, both of which (together with the Vere Scholarship Fund) owe their origin to one of the earliest of these charitable bequests, that of Raines Waite in 1694. Manning School, named for its founder, was established in 1738 at Savanna-la-Mar. At Lucea is Rusea's School, and at Port Antonio the Titchfield School. Wolmer's School which was started in 1736, owes its beginning to a Kingston goldsmith of that name who left by his will £2360 for the founding of a free school. Beckford and Smith's School in Spanish Town (now the St Jago High School for boys and girls) is the result of the combining of two separate bequests, the second of which was 'for the instruction of the poorer classes of all colours, free and slave, in the doctrines of the Church of England and in the promotion of industry'. Munro College and Hampton School for girls at Malvern were originally maintained by the Munro and Dickenson Trust, while Jamaica College, now at Hope, springs from the foundation made originally by Charles Drax for educating eight poor boys and four poor girls of the parish of St Ann. Actually, the money had to be recovered by a long drawn-out lawsuit from a member of the Beckford family who had managed to get hold of Drax's chief property. The school was started in 1795 in the old St Ann court house. It later became the Jamaica Free School at Walton, St Ann, being removed in 1885 to its present site, after a short stay in the Barbican great house near by.

Although these schools started as charity institutions, those that survive have done so as fee-paying grammar schools which are beyond the reach of poor children, except with government assistance. Significant expansion of educational opportunity began with the award of free places and grant-in-aid places at secondary level, and in 1973 the free education policy at secondary level was introduced. That year 4084 free places were awarded; by 1980 the number had risen to 8766. In the early 1970s fifty new junior secondary schools were built with the help of a loan from the World Bank. They offered the first three years of secondary education. In time it became necessary to convert these to secondary schools offering five years of secondary education. Today, primary education is free and in certain districts compulsory. A substantial part of the annual budget goes to the Ministry of Education. Considerable sums are devoted to the School of Agriculture, the College of Arts, Science and Technology, the University of the West Indies, the main campus of which is at Mona, a north-eastern section of Kingston, and teacher training colleges. Education is provided by government–aided and private schools, some of which are run by religious bodies.

Mico Training College, Kingston

With regard to the slaves, the only training they received was such as would increase or improve their labour. The majority learnt the business of cane cultivation in the field, generally under the driver; a few were trained in trades such as carpentry and cabinet making by craftsmen from Britain. The planters objected to any other form of learning for their slaves: only the missionaries thought they should be taught to read and write, but, although from as early as 1760 the Moravians were allowed to instruct the slaves in Christianity, they were forbidden to educate them otherwise, and the founding of schools had to wait until after emancipation.

An early and important step forward was the creation of schools for training teachers, money for which came from the Mico Trust in a rather romantic way. In 1670 Lady Mico left £1000 to be used to ransom any poor Christians who might be captured and enslaved by Algerian pirates of North Africa. In time the Mediterranean was cleared of these pirates and, with no more Christians to ransom, the money was invested and left to accumulate, until by 1827 it amounted to some £120 000! The question of what to do with this vast sum was solved by Sir Thomas Fowell Buxton who suggested that it be used for 'the promotion of education in the British Colonies'. The suggestion was accepted, schools were opened in various islands and teachers' training colleges founded in Jamaica and Antigua. The Mico College in Jamaica came at the right time; it assisted in training the first batch of teachers after emancipation and set the pattern for the four women's training colleges – Shortwood, St Joseph's, Bethlehem and Moneague. Today there are eight teacher colleges – Bethlehem, Church, Mico, Moneague, Passley Gardens, St Joseph's, Sam Sharpe and Shortwood – all, with the exception of Shortwood, co-educational.

139

It was to the Churches that the main burden of organising education and setting up schools fell after 1838. They were assisted at the start by yearly grants from England and later by money voted by the Jamaica government. But in the conditions which existed during the 'dark age' not enough was achieved. The provision made was small and poor in quality. More schools and teachers were needed. In education, as in so many other sides of life, it took the events of 1865 to bring about the much needed improvements.

But neglect had produced its results in the form of ignorance: in 1883 only 22 000 blacks out of the quarter million in the island could write. By 1892 elementary education was free and within four years the total number of schools in the island stood at 900, or twice what it had been in 1866. Actually, it was found advisable later to combine many of these schools with larger and more efficient ones. The Infant School movement and the development of technical education also had their beginnings about this time.

Jamaica's dependencies

It was during the Crown Colony period that most of Jamaica's dependencies were formally acquired and that proper arrangements governing their relationship with the island were made. These dependent territories were the Cayman Islands, the Turks and Caicos group and the Pedro and Morant Cays.

The Cayman Islands, settled mainly by English from Jamaica, had always been regarded as under the control of the governor of Jamaica, but were not formally attached until 1863. The islands were administered by a Commissioner assisted by a legislative body known as the Justices and Vestry, all laws passed having to be approved by the governor of Jamaica. This relationship was to cease when Jamaica attained independence; and the islands are now a British colony. Called by Columbus *Las Tortugas*[1] because of the abundance of turtles he found there, turtle fishing has remained for long one of the main industries. Boat-building is another occupation for which the islanders are noted.

Lying some 700 kilometres north-east of Jamaica, the Turks and Caicos group were first settled by people from Bermuda who went there to rake salt, still a major industry. Although geographically a part of the Bahamas, these islands asked to be treated for administrative purposes as separate from the group in 1848, being (also at their request) formally attached to Jamaica as a dependency in 1874. This relationship ceased also when Jamaica became independent, and today the islands are a British colony. The Turks and Caicos have their own governor but they share with the Bahamas a common bench in their Court of Appeal.

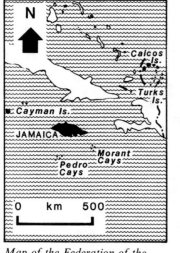

Map of the Federation of the Turks and Caicos Islands

[1] The present name – a Carib word for alligator – was given, some say, because the early settlers found alligators there; others, because Grand Cayman (the largest island in the group) is shaped like an alligator.

The Morant and Pedro Cays were officially annexed by Jamaica in 1882. The four small islets making up the former group lie 50 kilometres southeast of Morant Point. The Pedro Cays, four in number also, are some 70 kilometres south of Pedro Bluff, St Elizabeth. The cays are chiefly valuable as fishing centres, and for the eggs laid there by sea birds and sold in the island as 'booby eggs'. *Guano*, the droppings of these birds, is used as a fertiliser.

The banana industry

In 1870 one of Sir John Peter Grant's most important schemes was started – the Rio Cobre Irrigation Works – for providing the dry lands lying near to Spanish Town with water. The rainfall on the St Catherine plain is one of the lowest in the island, and before the irrigation works were built only land very close to the foothills could be used for cane cultivation. The scheme, completed in six years, barely paid its way at the start because, with the exception of the proprietors of Caymanas and of one or two neighbouring estates, none of the property owners in the area considered it worthwhile to cultivate cane or other crops, and used only enough water to irrigate their guinea grass pastures. A change soon came with the development of the banana industry and, later, the revival of sugar. Today thousands of hectares of land are under irrigation, for which provision the government earns a not inconsiderable revenue.

Although sugar production in the Crown Colony period was expanding in places like Trinidad and Guyana, in Jamaica few planters cultivated the crop. The chief reason for this was the unwillingness of labourers to work on the Jamaica estates, and even if they were prepared to work the cane farmers did not have the money to pay them. In 1848 there were over 500 estates in operation, in 1910 about 70 – but the population, meanwhile, had grown steadily. Provision crops helped to solve the resulting problem, and the export of rum, tobacco, ginger, pimento and a little citrus brought in some money, but this was not enough: Jamaica's economic future had begun to look most uncertain when the banana trade came to the rescue.

Originating in South Asia, the banana is believed to have been carried across Africa by the Arabs. It was taken from the Canary Islands to Hispaniola in 1516 by a Spanish missionary and from Hispaniola introduced into Jamaica. The name *banana* covers a large family of plants including the plantain; other distant relatives are the travellers' palm, ginger and the canna. Cultivation of the banana is very ancient and its fruit was one of man's first foods.

There are many varieties of banana, but that for which Jamaica became famous and on which the industry here was founded was what is now called the Gros Michel, 'Gros' because of the largeness of the plant and its fruit. This variety was brought into the island by a French botanist named Pouyat from Martinique and first planted at his St Andrew coffee property Bel Air. Because of its place of origin, this banana was for a long time known to the country people as *martnick*.

The banana had always been grown in the island on a small scale and eaten locally, but no one imagined until early in the Crown Colony period that it could become an export crop, let alone one that was to rival sugar in value. One of the first attempts at carrying bananas to the United States was made in 1866 by Captain George Busch, when he took aboard a small cargo of the fruit at Oracabessa and Port Antonio and sold it at a profit fourteen days later in Boston. For some time he had been carrying Cuban-grown bananas to America, but discovering that the Jamaican fruit was superior he had made this trial trip to the island. He early recognised the suitability of the country round about Port Antonio for banana growing and on later trips went from district to district urging the small settlers to grow the fruit. Originally banana cultivation was beneath the dignity of the big planters.

The real beginning of the banana export trade, however, dates from the voyage made four years later by Captain Lorenzo Dow Baker, then master of an 85-tonne sailing ship. Learning of the good quality and plentiful supply of Jamaican bananas, he decided to call here on one of his trips to New York from Central America and investigate. He took on a small cargo of bananas at Port Morant for which he paid a shilling a bunch. After a quick trip north he sold them at a profit. He returned the following year and at Port Antonio loaded a full cargo of coconuts and bananas, which he again managed to land in good condition.

There was no doubt now as to the possibility of developing the fruit trade. In 1879 Baker became agent for a newly-formed shipping company and so secured the vessels needed to carry the bananas from Jamaica to the United States. In those days, before refrigeration, the success of a trip depended on the speed with which it could be made. Any delay gave the fruit time to become over-ripe and spoil before it was delivered, as happened on many of the trips Baker (and the company that had been formed around him) undertook. The risk was reduced by the use of steam freighters, which were soon put on the banana shipping route, and of ice refrigeration.

A number of the older fruit companies now began to find themselves losing business to the Baker concern and agreed to sell out to it. This reorganisation resulted in the formation of the Boston Fruit Company. The new company's first two years of trading proved extremely profitable and it was decided to use part of the profits to purchase properties for banana cultivation. Bog, near Port Antonio, and Bowden Estates, Port Morant, were the first purchased.

Meanwhile in Costa Rica a thriving fruit trade to New York was being developed by the Keith and Lindo families, and other companies were operating successfully in Cuba and the Dominican Republic. In 1899 the United Fruit Company of New Jersey was formed, which cleared the way of almost all rivals by buying out the Boston Fruit Company, the Keith interests and some dozen other small companies to become the biggest and most important banana concern in the world. An English steamship company formed two years later to provide ships, fitted with refrigeration, for carrying bananas to England and Europe was immediately employed by the United Fruit Company, and later bought out by them.

Banana cultivation, as we have seen, started in the Port Antonio area of Portland where the soil and heavy rainfall were especially suitable. It early brought some prosperity to the area. Soon cultivation began to spread west, then south, even into the sugar lands, where in places it replaced the cane. It was a crop which could be grown with profit by all types of cultivators; even the small settler with only a couple of hectares of land grew some bananas which he sold to commission agents at railway stations. Furthermore, unlike sugar production which gives employment to most of its workers at certain seasons only, bananas can be harvested throughout the year. Another feature of the banana business was that it created a large fleet that carried passengers and freight, as well as fruit. These ships were for a long time the only regular means of travel between Jamaica and many other lands.

An interesting and important development of this period, in Jamaica and the West Indies generally, was the tendency for primary producers, that is, the growers of the main crops, to come together and form themselves into associations for mutual protection and benefit. This tendency showed itself early in the banana industry. In 1929 the Jamaica Banana Producers Association was formed to knit growers together into one body for protection and cooperative action. This development, together with the stable conditions which existed in the island – the authority of the government, and respect for law – protected the independence of the banana growers and prevented outside companies, even one as powerful as the United Fruit Company, from getting exclusive control of the trade. In less settled and developed countries such companies managed by various means to have their own way, but this was never really possible in Jamaica. Within two years of its formation the Jamaica Banana Producers Association was handling a very large part of the island's total output of fruit, and, with government help, running a regular shipping service. In 1936 the Association became a private trading company, but is still very largely owned by and identified with the banana growers of the island and serves their interests along with the All Island Banana Growers Association, itself another primary producer organisation.

The same tendency to form groups for the protection of common interests and the securing of common benefits resulted in the formation of associations of cane farmers, citrus, cocoa, coffee and coconut producers and livestock breeders, which have proved to be of social as well as economic importance. Closely connected with these associations are the cooperative groups and credit societies.

The sugar and banana trades have played at seesaw in Jamaica: often as the one rose in volume and importance, the other sank. Both World Wars I and II encouraged sugar production, but brought the banana industry close to ruin, and, on both occasions, at times when the latter had reached a high point in value. The export of bananas almost ceased during World War II owing to the lack of shipping and the unimportance of the fruit when compared with other types of food. Fortunately the British government generously paid for each year's crop, although it was never shipped, and so protected both the banana industry and economy of the island.

Bananas are a risky crop to grow, for the plants are soft and easily blown down by a strong wind. A hurricane will flatten whole fields. Still, the crop is a quick one and within a year another is ready for reaping. Today insurance against such loss gives the grower protection, but in the old days hurricane damage was accepted as a part of the business, and as there were more good years than bad, for more than half a century the banana proved to be the island's agricultural standby.

What brought far greater harm to the industry than anything else, especially in the late 1930s, were the diseases that began to attack the plants. The two most serious and widespread are the Panama Disease and Leaf Spot, both of which came from Central America. The former is by far the more deadly. It spreads rapidly through the soil from plant to plant, causing severe wilting and rapid death. The disease leaves the soil infected and unfit for future cultivation for many years. The damage caused by Leaf Spot has been controlled by spraying and the development of varieties of fruit, such as the Lacatan which is highly resistant to Panama disease, and not as susceptible to Leaf Spot as the Gros Michel. These two diseases posed a grave threat to the banana industry and have already affected it greatly. This is disturbing, for bananas are necessary to the island. No other crop has done more for the general raising of the economic conditions of the people: it has helped a large number of small farmers to acquire their own holdings, and encouraged the formation of a strong and independent peasantry which would not, perhaps, have been possible otherwise.

A revival in sugar

The seesaw, fortunately, was in motion again, and the period that saw the decline of the banana witnessed the surprising recovery of sugar – the old staple crop of the West Indies. This revival was started by the West Indies Sugar Company, a subsidiary of Messrs Tate and Lyle Investments Limited, of England. They bought up a number of properties in the island, including some that had belonged to the United Fruit Company, and started growing sugar on a big scale. The process was greatly helped by improved methods of production and the development of the big modern factory to do the work that a number of small, inefficient factories did before. This resulted in a greatly increased yield of sugar cane per hectare. In 1888 the average yield was 45 tonnes, in 1956 it was 81. Another interesting development was the change in the pattern of production. Originally a crop grown on large plantations only, today a high percentage of the canes ground comes from the small farmer with a two-hectare plot.

Migration

A feature of the Crown Colony period was the beginning of migration from the island of thousands of workers. This new development was brought about largely by the attraction of outside jobs, and made possible by improved transport. It was to affect in many ways the life and thought of the new Jamaica.

The first wave of migration was to Panama in the 1860s to help build the railway there. The French attempt to cut a canal across the isthmus in 1879 again drew Jamaican workers to Panama. The company which undertook the project had been formed under Ferdinand de Lesseps, French diplomat and creator of the Suez Canal joining the Mediterranean and Red Seas. The project failed, owing largely to the effects of yellow fever among the workers. European employees died like flies from the disease, as did the Chinese labourers brought in to dig the canal. Jamaicans, and West Indians generally, stood up better to the fever, but a great many died nevertheless. Within nine years, after a shocking waste of life and money, the canal scheme collapsed. No arrangements were made to send back the Jamaicans to the island or provide for them in any way, and most stayed there and shifted for themselves as best they could.

The successful American attempt in the 1900s to build the canal again drew large numbers of Jamaicans. Convinced of the need, mainly for military reasons, for a shorter sea route between the Atlantic and Pacific coasts than that round Cape Horn at the tip of South America, Theodore Roosevelt, then President of the United States, set about buying the rights of the French canal company. Panama was at that time a province of Colombia, but with Roosevelt's secret support and approval it broke away from Colombia and became a republic on its own which granted the United States a strip of land 16 kilometres wide along the canal route.

By that time it had at last been discovered that yellow fever was caused by the bite of a certain species of mosquito, so a systematic attack on the mosquitoes on the isthmus banished the disease that had helped defeat de Lesseps. Jamaica, largest and nearest of the West Indian islands, furnished most of the labourers needed for the project, and in the ten years which it took to complete, Colón became a half-Jamaican town. Many of the migrants stayed on when the canal was completed, and their descendants are there in large numbers to this day. Some sent for relatives to come and join them or to visit, many travelled back and forth, and still others returned home when the job was done, better off than when they left Jamaica and with a certain swagger about them which became the subject of a popular song, *Colon Man*:

> *Colon man da come, Colon man da come,*
> *Brass chain da lick him belly bam, bam, bam;*
> *But if you ask him fe de time*
> *Him look upon de sun!*

Up to 1930 the greater number of foreign workers in Panama came from Jamaica and it was mainly Jamaica again that supplied labour for the Canal Zone in World War II.

The development of the banana industry in Central America drew numbers of Jamaicans there. Along the coastlands they settled, working on the plantations in Costa Rica and Honduras, building homes and shops in towns like Limón and Cristóbal. Tougher, as a rule, and more hard-working than the natives, they found ready employment until with the coming of the bad economic conditions of the 1930s preference had to be given to local labour.

But other openings occurred in Cuba, and once more Jamaicans migrated in their thousands in search of work on the sugar and coffee plantations. Here too, in time, the flood of outside workers into the country was checked in the interests of the local worker, but, as in Panama, in Cuba today (in spite of the great number deported) there are many descendants of those early migrants who bravely went abroad in search of work.

Greater, perhaps, than the other migrations combined has been that to the United States which began as the nineteenth century drew to its end. The quota regulations which were to check this flow considerably did not operate then, and the migrant did not even need a passport to enter the country. Boston, the North American home port of the banana ships, was the place that attracted the migrants at first; later the drift was towards Baltimore, Philadelphia, New York, and more recently to the tri-state area of New York, New Jersey and Connecticut where there are some 350 000 resident Jamaicans. Those who went have followed most professions and trades.

Immigrants from the Caribbean to Britain, disembarking at Southampton in 1962

With the coming of World War II new opportunities for work in the United States were created for Jamaican and West Indian labourers in the form of contract jobs on farms. Otherwise the chances of emigration have become limited. This has had the effect of turning the tide towards Canada, but the tightening of restrictions there also caused the West Indian migrant to look towards the United Kingdom.

Although what is called *primary migration* began in 1943, movement in this direction was unimportant before the early 1950s. Small numbers had gone during the war as munition and factory workers, and about 8000 joined the armed services, but between 1950–60 some 200 000 Jamaicans entered Britain. The tightening up of immigration laws in the 1960s resulted in a dramatic decrease in migration, so much so that from 1971–73 only 9000 West Indians (the majority of whom were Jamaicans) entered Britain. Primary migration has now ended, except for children joining relatives already settled there and husbands and wives going to their spouses.

In spite of the decline of sugar, the development of the banana industry and the migration which took place during the Crown Colony regime contributed to an economic recovery that was to be interrupted by two events of this period: the earthquake of 1907, and the world war that broke out seven years later – although the latter, as we have seen, helped the revival of the sugar industry.

The 1907 earthquake

The earthquake which shook most of Kingston to its foundations, occurred at about 3.30 p.m. on 14 January. The shock, felt throughout the island and in neighbouring countries as well, wrecked some buildings in Lower St Andrew, Port Royal, [1] Buff Bay and Spanish Town; but it was in Kingston, near which the earthquake was centred, that the greatest damage was done.

Without warning a series of tremendous shocks, lasting less than half a minute in all, brought most of the brick and mortar city crashing down in ruins and crushing to death or burying alive a thousand people. To add to the horror and the number of dead, fires broke out that raged through the stricken town for more than four days, hampering rescue operations and completing the destruction of much that the earthquake had spared or only slightly damaged, and bringing the loss of property to more than £2 000 000.

Dazed and terrified, most of the survivors fled to the Parade Gardens, the Race Course and other open spaces, where they spent that first awful night, and many more to come. In the Parade Gardens a curious sight, which probably remained unnoticed at first, was the statue of Queen Victoria, turned almost completely round by the earthquake's spinning motion, but still standing upright on its pedestal.

[1] The old Royal Artillery Store, better known as the 'Giddy House', still leans at a crazy angle from the earthquake's effect.

The public hospital was strained to the limit to care for the hundreds of injured people brought in. As for the dead, some were given proper burial in churchyards, but many had to be disposed of in large trenches in the May Pen cemetery and a number burnt with little ceremony.

Taking advantage of the confusion, looters began to rob stores, houses and even the dead and dying lying about. The posting of armed guards throughout the city by the Governor, Sir James Swettenham, and other prompt measures, soon checked the looting, but out of this an unfortunate incident was to develop. Three days after the earthquake, three American warships, under Admiral C. H. Davis, arrived from Guantánamo Bay, Cuba, bringing doctors and medical supplies. This much-needed assistance, and the help given by working-parties of sailors, was deeply appreciated. Largely at the request of the American Vice-Consul, however, a small party of armed marines was landed to guard the Consulate and its records. This should not have been done without permission from the government and Swettenham requested Admiral Davis to withdraw his marines. Offended by this, the Admiral sailed away with the supplies he had brought. A personal gift of 2000 tonnes of beef and other foodstuffs from President Theodore Roosevelt to the people of Kingston, then on its way to the island, was, on Davis's orders, returned to Cuba as soon as the ship on which it had been sent arrived here. The incident was soon magnified in importance and Swettenham was requested by the Colonial Office to apologise to Admiral Davis. He did so, but at the same time resigned as Governor. He was succeeded in May by Sir Sidney (later Baron) Olivier,[1] the most energetic governor the island had had since Sir John Peter Grant.

Relief work quickly got under way with the appointment of a committee with Archbishop Enos Nuttall as chairman. Supplies of food and clothing were collected and distributed and temporary housing put up to shelter some of the homeless. Recovery was greatly aided by a very generous gift and loan from the British government, and by the fund opened by the Lord Mayor of London to which over £55 000 was contributed.

The insurance held on property in Kingston did not cover damage from fire caused by earthquake. The policyholders claimed, however, that the fire had started just *before* the earthquake when a maid upset a bunsen burner in a doctor's office on King Street. After a long and keenly fought lawsuit, the juries found in favour of the policyholders and the insurance companies were forced to pay nearly £1 000 000 in compensation.

With all this money the rebuilding of Kingston was assured and a new and safer city from the point of view of earthquakes, soon rose from the ruins of the old. Although much improved in many respects, the new town plan followed the old too closely: the planners did not expect the city to grow as it has, nor did they reckon on the effects of motor traffic.

On 1 March 1957, almost exactly fifty years after Kingston's destruction, an earthquake, the heaviest since that of 1907, shook the island. Its effects were greatest in the western parishes where a few lives were lost and severe damage done to property. Among the buildings wrecked was the

[1] He wrote two well-known books on the island, *The Myth of Governor Eyre*. London, 1933; and *Jamaica: The Blessed Island*. London, 1936.

ancient St James Parish Church, Montego Bay. In Port Royal a narrow strip of coast 180 metres long disappeared beneath the sea – a grim reminder of what occurred in 1692.

The First World War

Although the great war of 1914 to 1918 was fought thousands of kilometres from Jamaica, its effects were strongly felt in the island. In fact, few countries, if any, were not involved in one way or another. The events which led to the war are too complicated to relate here. Matters came to a head with the invasion by Germany of France (a country with which Britain was allied) and of Belgium (which Britain was pledged to protect). On the 4 August 1914, Great Britain declared war on Germany.

The effects of that war on the banana and sugar industries have been mentioned. The life of the island was to be affected in other ways as well. Eager to play their part in the fighting, some 11 000 men in all from Jamaica went to the front, many of whom died on active service. Although a Conscription Law was passed in 1917 by which males from 16 to 41 years of age became liable for military service, it was never put into force: all the recruits needed joined of their own free will. The first contingent of men sailed in November 1915. Ten others were to follow. They helped form eleven battalions of the newly-raised British West Indies Regiment whose record in the terrible war worthily upheld the reputation gained in former days by the old West India Regiment.

This latter regiment has a long, exciting history that goes back to the War of American Independence. It was first formed out of a number of corps (consisting of white and black loyalists) of which the South Carolina Corps was one. After many reorganisations and changes of name, the force became known as the West India Regiment. Its battle record is a proud one. West India Regiments (there were twelve at one time) took an active part in the fierce fighting throughout the West Indies during the Napoleonic Wars, and later on, in operations on the West African Coast, notably in the Ashanti Wars of 1864 and 1873–4. Two soldiers of the regiment won the Victoria Cross for outstanding acts of bravery. They were Private Samuel Hodge of the 4th West India Regiment who gained his award in 1866, and Sergeant William James Gordon, twenty-six years later. Gordon lived until 1922 and was buried in the cemetery at Up Park Camp with full military honours. The zouave uniform was adopted by the corps at the suggestion of Queen Victoria. In 1926 the regiment, with the exception of the band, was dismissed from service for reasons of economy. With the federation of the British West Indian Territories, the regiment was re-formed on a regional basis for the defence and internal security of the area.

Chapter 19

The road to self-government

The Morant Bay rebellion gave Eyre the excuse he needed to recommend openly that the old constitution of the island be abolished. He had more than once privately suggested such a course to the Colonial Office, which, however, did not wish to take action in the matter until it knew it would have the full support of a strong party in the House of Assembly. It must be admitted that the Assembly and Legislative Council had not been making a success of governing, and after the Morant Bay trouble willingly gave up control.

There are various kinds of Crown Colony government[1]. When the entire legislature is nominated by the Crown it is pure Crown Colony government. Such a system existed in Jamaica until 1884. From then, till 1944, the island had a semi-representative government – that is, the legislature was partly elected and partly nominated, but it was a form of Crown Colony administration, nevertheless.

The new system was designed for efficiency and quick action. At its centre stood the governor, armed with enough power to push through any reasonable measures. The reforms of Sir John Peter Grant, first of these governors, and the efforts of his successors to carry forward his policies, were mentioned in the previous chapter. These reforms were necessary and long overdue, and it is regrettable that they had not been brought about earlier by a government representative of the people. Grant himself was a hearty, cheerful sort of man and got along well with almost everyone. So at the start all classes were satisfied with the new system. To the ruling class it brought freedom from fear of the political rise of the educated coloured people, who, on their part, felt that the change of government had prevented further possible unrest and bloodshed, which would have affected them as well as the black peasants, who in turn, in a confused sort of way regarded the change, following as it did the Morant Bay trouble, as an effort by the Queen's government to protect them.

There was, as we know, a small group that had opposed the surrender of the constitution. The group never really changed its views, even amidst the

[1]See chapter 16.

King's House, Jamaica, as it was in the late nineteenth century

early blessings that flowed from the new government, and as time went on its numbers grew. The first cause of widespread criticism to which the new system gave rise was the high cost of developments and the sharp increase in taxes necessary to meet the cost. But, as the governor was the government, there was little anyone else could do but complain. The newspapers, generally favourable at first to the government, soon changed their tune. 'Taken all in all we regard the Legislative Council as a sham', declared the *Morning Journal* as early as February 1867; adding, some time later, 'Why not shut the doors . . . and issue the laws from King's House?'

So opposition grew. Sir William Grey succeeded Grant, being himself followed by Sir Anthony Musgrave[1] in 1877. Musgrave became entangled in a lawsuit for illegally detaining a ship called the *Florence* because he suspected that she was engaged in contraband traffic. When the damages were charged to him personally as governor, he, on instructions from London, ordered that it be paid out of Jamaica's public funds. There was strong opposition to this, but in the end the Legislative Council was forced to agree to the payment of half the costs, the British government paying the other half.

[1] An avenue in Kingston and a street in St Ann's Bay were named after him, and Lady Musgrave Road, St Andrew, after his wife, an able social worker who founded the now defunct Women's Self-Help Society in Kingston.

The *Florence* case is important, first as an illustration of the methods of pure Crown Colony administration; and also because it was not until the political crisis which grew out of the case that the demands then being voiced for constitutional change became strong enough to make the Colonial Office act. Some of the opponents of the system were men who had approved the surrendering of the old: they now admitted their mistake. In 1883 Sir Henry Norman was sent out as governor with a slightly advanced form of constitution which was put into effect the following year. Under it the Legislative Council was now to consist of the governor, nine nominated and nine elected members. Whatever say this gave the elected part of the government in the running of affairs was, however, made valueless by the fact that the governor could always fall back on what was known as his reserved powers to have his own way, providing he felt that so doing was of paramount importance to the colony. Eleven years later the number of elected members was increased to 14 – one for each parish – but they had no more power than had the 9 before them.

The pace of progress under the Crown Colony system depended to a large extent on the type of governor sent out. Sir Henry Blake, for example, who arrived in 1889, had his term of office extended at the people's request. He built roads and bridges and arranged the successful 1891 Exhibition in Kingston.[1] His relations with the Legislative Council were good; on the other hand those of his successor, Sir Augustus Hemming, were unsuccessful. Still, with all its faults, much was achieved under the Crown Colony system. The main drawback was the way in which these achievements came about: government was imposed from on top, a system under which no people would ever learn to govern themselves.

Although in these conditions the political life of the island seemed almost stagnant, below the surface changes were at work. One was the part the black section of the community was beginning to play in public affairs. This was encouraged by the efforts of a gifted black man, Dr Robert Love. By the beginning of the twentieth century he had helped a black candidate to be elected to the Council and himself won a seat in 1906. By the 1920s there were more black members than white; by the 1930s the membership was almost entirely black. A similar change was taking place in the Civil Service where several black officers had started careers which were to take them to top posts in their departments.

The part played by Marcus Garvey in other ways was also an important one. He left Jamaica as a youth for the United States. There he started the Universal Negro Improvement Association, with the object of bettering the condition of Negroes everywhere and establishing a government for them in Africa. Deported from the United States after serving a prison sentence for fraud in connection with the Black Star Steamship Line which he had founded, he returned to Jamaica in 1927 to continue his work here. Although nothing much came of his schemes, Garvey himself, a strong and colourful personality, acquired a powerful hold on the imagination of the mass of the people and did much to create unity among blacks and give

[1]The exhibition which ran from January to May, was held in a large building, erected for the purpose, on the present site of the Wolmer's School. It was opened by Prince George afterwards King George the Fifth.

Marcus Garvey, National Hero of Jamaica

them a pride in their race. Later political leaders were to profit from the lessons of Garvey's career. Garvey died in London in 1940 and was buried there. He was later declared a National Hero of Jamaica and his remains were brought back to the island and interred in National Heroes Park.

From 1900 onwards criticism of the island's government, especially by elected members of the Council led by the barrister J. A. G. Smith, grew so strong that in 1921 a Commission from the Colonial Office under Major E. F. L. Wood (later Lord Halifax), was sent out to examine the situation at first hand. The Commission recommended further constitutional changes which, as it happened, were not regarded in Jamaica as far-reaching enough, but the offer was rejected for other reasons. And so time dragged on. Meanwhile forces were building up in Jamaica (and in the West Indies generally) which, coupled with the trend of world events, were to produce many and surprising changes.

A worldwide industrial depression which began in 1929 and caused great distress in Britain and the United States, early affected the West Indies. A fall in the prices of all raw products, plus competition from the European beet-sugar industry now recovered from the effects of World War I, had disastrous results on the West Indian sugar trade, at a time too when the Jamaica banana industry had started to decline. Migration opportunities became very limited: in fact, thousands of Jamaicans were being sent back. But the population had greatly increased, wages were low, there was less work for more people, and the government was too poor to help.

The 1938 disorders

These conditions, and the suffering and discontent which grew out of them, were general throughout the islands, but nowhere were the labouring classes organised in unions for common action and the orderly presentation of demands for better conditions. Although as early as 1919 the Jamaica waterfront workers had two registered unions, twenty years were to pass before a proper trade union movement developed. Labour trouble started in 1935 when St Kitts sugar workers struck for more wages. Unorganised strikes, with bloodshed, broke out in Barbados and Trinidad, in St Vincent, St Lucia and elsewhere. Jamaica's turn came early in 1938 with a strike at the West Indies Sugar Company's estate Frome, in Westmoreland. Some of the strikers were killed in clashes with the police, many were injured, and damage done to canefields by fire. This was followed by serious disorders in Kingston and other parts of the island, and the arrest and short imprisonment of Alexander (later Sir Alexander) Bustamante who had emerged as the leader of the new labour movement. In the midst of the trouble the Governor, Sir Edward Denham, died (largely, it is thought, from worry over the state of affairs), and Sir Arthur Richards, a stern administrator with experience in the East, was appointed to deal with the situation.

These disorders mark an important stage in the history of the West Indies. Out of them came the first lasting labour unions, and the formation

The Daily Gleaner.

4 DEAD! 9 IN HOSPITAL!! 89 IN JAIL!!!

POLICE FORCED TO SHOOT DOWN RIOTERS IN WESTMORELAND

Dollar A Day Demand Ends In Deaths!

Part of The Daily Gleaner's *front page of 3 May, 1938, with accounts of the riot in Westmoreland*

of political parties linked with the unions. The first of these in Jamaica was Bustamante's Industrial Trade Union, later to be associated with the Labour Party formed by him. In 1938 Norman Manley, the island's foremost barrister and a cousin of Bustamante, launched the socialist People's National Party, later to be closely linked with the Trades Union Council, and, more recently, with the National Workers' Union. Manley and Bustamante are now National Heroes of Jamaica.

The rise of labour to political power was a new and dramatic development in the West Indies, and its leaders pressed not only for increased wages but for political reform as well. Whereas the earlier dissatisfaction with Crown Colony government had been met by gradual constitutional changes, the demand now was for the abolition of the system itself and the granting of responsible government.

Concerned by the disturbances in the West Indies, a Royal Commission headed by Lord Moyne, was sent out by the Colonial Office to inquire into the state of the islands. It toured the area and gathered a mass of evidence. Before its report was published, however, the peace of the world was shattered once more and Great Britain found herself again at war with Germany.

The Second World War

The war affected Jamaica in a number of ways. The effects on trade and industry have been already mentioned.

As before, a number of men and women joined the armed services, and contingents were formed for local defence. In 1940 several air and naval bases in the British West Indies were leased to the United States by Britain. Those in Jamaica were situated mainly in the area around Portland Bight.

The war had the effect of drawing attention to the West Indies. This was partly the result of growing criticism of Britain's treatment of dependent colonies, and partly from concern over the bad conditions brought to light by the Royal Commission. In 1940 a summary of the Commission's recommendations was published and that same year the first Colonial Development and Welfare Act was passed by which assistance to the extent of £5 000 000 a year for ten years and £500 000 for research and inquiry was voted by Parliament. A special *Comptroller for Development and Welfare*, with a technical and research staff, was appointed for the West Indies with headquarters in Barbados, to assist the governments in framing schemes to be paid for from C. D. & W. grants. These steps were outstanding acts of faith, for in 1940 the future could scarcely have been more uncertain. France had fallen to the Germans, Britain was enduring frightful air attacks and the chances of victory seemed all on the side of Germany. The second C. D. & W. Act, passed five years later, increased the money available for the colonies to £120 000 000 for ten years.

The establishment of a Colonial Development Corporation, and in 1942 of the Anglo-American Caribbean Commission – later extended to include the French and Dutch and reorganised as the Caribbean Commission – with headquarters in Port-of-Spain, Trinidad, were also to play an important part in providing a framework for the long-needed social and economic development of the area as a whole.

The road to self-government

The attention drawn by the events of the 1930s, and influenced also by the war, increased the rate of political change in the West Indies. In Jamaica this resulted in the New Constitution of 20 November 1944, by which the Crown Colony period was brought to an end and the island placed securely on the road to self-government. It provided for two chambers in the Legislature, the first called the House of Representatives, composed of thirty-two elected members; the other, the Legislative Council, a nominated body consisting of official and unofficial members. It provided also for the setting up of an Executive Council, composed of the Governor as Chairman, with three officials and two nominated unofficials, and five members (called Ministers) elected by the House of Representatives.

The inclusion of full adult suffrage, that is, the right of all males and females twenty-one years and over (now reduced to eighteen) to vote at elections, was not generally favoured because of the island's high illiteracy rate, but was adopted nevertheless. Its adoption was in great measure owing to the efforts of Norman Manley and the People's National Party. To them also belongs the credit for popularising the doctrine of self-government when such an idea was remote and unpopular in other quarters.

The inclusion of full adult suffrage was a long step forward. As we have seen, in the early days the vote was limited to white freeholders. Even after emancipation, and in spite of the efforts of the Colonial Office, the island's ruling class found ways of restricting the numbers of people who could vote. Although a low property qualification with a literacy test was established in 1885, and female suffrage granted thirty-four years later, in 1938 only about one-twelfth of the population could vote. A census taken in January 1943 showed the population as 1 237 063, of whom some 700 000 were now eligible for a vote: under the old system fewer than 20 000 had qualified. The power to elect the representatives of their choice had at last become the right of the people – a right and a responsibility.

The first elections under the new constitution, held shortly after its proclamation, were run on a party basis. This was also a new development. Although from the earliest days of civil government members of the House of Assembly took a vigorous and often violent part in the political disputes of the time, there were no political parties in the modern sense: the usual understanding being that all elected members were more or less opposed to the executive government and the officials.

The Jamaica Labour Party and People's National Party were the two main contestants. The elections resulted in a sweeping victory for the J.L.P. which won 25 seats out of a total of 32 in the House of Representatives. The party lost some ground in the years that followed and at the second general election, held in 1949, won, but by a reduced majority.

The 1944 Constitution – the most advanced at the time in the British West Indies – was useful for its period. It provided a system under which official, nominated and elected members were expected to take joint responsibility for the making of policy and the carrying out of executive government. But it had weaknesses; one of these was that while the so-called ministers were expected to deal in Executive Council with the whole range of government activities and to answer in the House of Representatives for various subjects and government departments, they had no executive responsibility over these departments. By 1951 when Sir Hugh Foot arrived as governor, it was felt that the time had come for a further increase in the island's constitutional powers. Discussions held that year with the two political parties and with the unofficial members of the Legislative Council led to the introduction in June 1953 of important changes in the constitution.

These provided for the appointment of a Chief Minister and seven other Ministers (all drawn from the House of Representatives) so increasing from five to eight the number of House of Representative members in the Executive Council, and giving them a majority over the official and nominated members. This was a vitally important change since ministers could now exercise wide responsibility in the management of the internal

Norman Manley, one time premier of Jamaica and leader of the West Indies Federal Labour Party

affairs of the island, and, for the first time, enjoy executive functions in regard to the various departments of the government. The only limit placed on the powers and authority of the Ministers was in respect of public security and matters affecting the members of the Civil Service (for which the Colonial Secretary remained responsible), and public prosecutions (the responsibility of the Attorney-General).

Under the new system Alexander Bustamante became the island's first Chief Minister. At the general election held early in 1955, however, the People's National Party won a majority in the House and its leader, Norman Manley, took over as head of the government.

Within two years – on 11 November 1957 – further constitutional changes providing for Cabinet Government and virtual internal self-rule were inaugurated.

The Executive Council was now replaced by a Cabinet called the Council of Ministers and presided over by the Chief Minister. It consisted of eight or nine members from the House of Representatives, and two or three from the Legislative Council, in each case appointed by the Governor on the recommendation of the Chief Minister. Official members no longer had a place on the Council, and the Colonial Secretary (now called Chief Secretary) and the Financial Secretary lost their seats on the Legislative Council. The Governor, for most constitutional purposes, was rapidly becoming a figurehead.

A 1960s picture of the House of Representatives, Kingston, Jamaica

The change of government necessitated the appointment of a Minister of Home Affairs, to take over most of the matters previously dealt with by the Colonial Secretary and some formerly the responsibility of the Attorney-General – a post necessary to the achievement of full internal self-government since its provision meant that for the first time security and justice became a purely local responsibility.

But these changes, far-reaching as they were, were regarded as interim to an even further revision of the Constitution to provide for full self-government. A special committee of the House was appointed to undertake the revision. Its report, tabled in April 1958, recommended that only bills relating to defence and international relations be reserved for the special assent of the Queen; that the Legislative Council be enlarged from 15 to 21 members; that no official should be a member of the Council of Ministers (this provision meaning, in effect, the removal of the Attorney-General, the only remaining official member of the Council); that the Council itself, renamed the Cabinet, should consist of not more than 15 members; that all reserved powers be removed from the Constitution and that although the Governor's veto powers should remain, these, as in Canada and other Dominions of the Commonwealth, should be exercised only on the advice of the Cabinet.

The first general elections under the new self-governing constitution, took place on 28 July 1959. It resulted in a decisive second-term victory for the People's National Party.

Chapter 20

Towards Independence

In following the course of the island's rapid constitutional advances during the 1950s, we have run somewhat ahead of the main narrative. It would be helpful to stop at this point to trace briefly the other developments which helped to make those in the constitutional field feasible – the development of natural resources, the growth of nationalism, and the experiment of a closer association with the other units of the British Caribbean which was to result in the rise and fall of the West Indies Federation.

Natural resources

Although agriculture had so far been the island's mainstay, with sugar and bananas the most important export crops, during the 1950s the country's developing economy and the resulting increased prosperity of its people came to rest equally firmly on industry, especially bauxite mining.

The pattern in the early post-war years was set by companies which processed local raw materials for local sale; but, encouraged by 'incentive legislation' and an active Industrial Development Corporation (as well as a similar Corporation for agriculture), a new industrial pattern quickly took shape, with imported and local raw materials being used to produce goods for world export as well as for the domestic market. With capital investment in manufacturing running at a level between £4 000 000 and £5 000 000 per annum there could in fact be few comparable countries to have made such rapid progress with industrialisation as did Jamaica. A list of the factories that were built is outside the scope of this work; their products ranged from baseballs to ceramics, gypsum to textiles, pharmaceuticals to neon-lights, and testified to the growing diversification of the industries.

The enormous expansion of the tourist trade is a relatively recent development. The industry might be said to have started at the beginning of this century when the Elder Dempster Steamship company began to operate a fast line of steamers between Jamaica and England, carrying passengers as well as bananas. The Myrtle Bank and Constant Spring Hotels were bought and run by the company along with their passenger

Kingston's Straw Market, where visitors may buy from one of the straw stalls

service. But tourism was a haphazard business until the end of the last war when it began to grow into the pillar of the economy it was to become.

It is in the field of bauxite mining that the development of the island's natural resources was greatest. Bauxite, the ore from which aluminium is made, is found chiefly in the 'red earth' of the Jamaica countryside. A geological survey of the island reported as early as 1869 that this earth was principally a mixture of iron and alumina. The report attracted little interest at the time for the metal *aluminium* was then almost unknown. Commercial production did not begin until nineteen years later, and another fifty were to pass before the aluminium industry first turned its attention to Jamaican bauxite.

In 1942, the island's bauxite reserves were estimated at five million tonnes and within a few years mining companies began to buy up properties that had bauxite deposits on them and to construct plants for processing the ore. More recent estimates were to place the reserves of commercial bauxite at 500 to 600 million tonnes. By the mid-1950s the three companies operating in the island were extracting more than five million tonnes of the ore a year, with a production target of nine million or more, maintaining Jamaica's position as the then largest producer of bauxite in the world, and a major producer of alumina. As the result of a revision, early in 1957, of the original agreement between the government and the companies, there was a considerable increase in revenue in the form of taxes and royalties paid on the ore mined. In 1956–57 this amounted to £352 000; by 1960–61 the figure had risen to £3 700 000! Other increases were to come in time with other revisions, as well as the world recession of the early 1980s which was to have such grave consequences for the industry.

The areas in which bauxite is chiefly mined are those that were found in the past to be most suitable for cattle rearing. Since the island has but limited land suitable for this and agricultural purposes generally, it was important that the government should provide by law that the large areas of land acquired by the bauxite companies were not taken out of production and held merely as mineral reserves; and further, that the lands mined out were not left derelict but were restored as far as possible to their previous level of productivity. The companies operating in the country have fulfilled these requirements efficiently.

Mining for bauxite, a clay-like compound and the chief source of alumina

Nationalism

An important trend of development was the growth of nationalism, of a national consciousness resulting from the discovery, so to speak, of Jamaica by Jamaicans regardless of racial origin or colour. This national consciousness which runs so strongly today through so much of Jamaican and West Indian life has been of slow and relatively recent growth. This could hardly have been otherwise in view of the course which the history of the area followed. As has been pointed out, it explains why much of that history probably appears disjointed and even unreal to West Indians today, for most of the factors which have shaped it originated outside the area and their story has been told from the outsider's point of view.

Even the great social revolution of Emancipation, without which no such development of the people as a whole could have been possible, was, like the introduction of plantation slavery itself, imposed from without. Since then, however, and for some time before, Jamaicans were driven back upon their own social resources and forced to develop 'a consciousness of their own separate existence', and to take the steady strides towards nationhood.

The process of this development has been slow and very complex: a process which has by no means ended. To examine it fully here is impossible. Many of the factors in that development have, indeed, been mentioned in the preceding chapters, but it may be useful at this point to sketch again the broad outlines of the picture.

The introduction of sugar and slavery early produced a society consisting of a relatively few white proprietors, in whose hands were concentrated most of the wealth of the island and the management of affairs, and thousands of black slaves without property or civil rights. As shown often in these pages, the slaves did not accept their condition without a struggle and one of the chief difficulties which faced the European ruling class in all the West Indian islands was the effective control of the great slave majority.

The appearance in time of a coloured section of the population changed the social structure by creating a free coloured middle class with more opportunities for advancement than the black slaves but hampered nevertheless by civil disabilities. By the first quarter of the nineteenth century, these free coloured people had far outnumbered the pure whites and, in spite of the restrictions on them, had acquired a good deal of wealth and some influence. Themselves large slave-owners, they did not throw in their lot with the emancipation movement until they had won their own hard-fought battle for civil rights.

The power of the original ruling class of the island began to wane with the abolition of the slave trade, while emancipation ensured its inevitable collapse, despite the efforts made to stave this off.

The work of the Nonconformist missionaries during the difficult transition period following emancipation was of the first importance. It was they who had brought Christianity to the slaves before freedom came, and to them fell the main burden of education for long after. It was the missionaries also who aided and encouraged the establishment of free villages, the settling of the black population on the land, and the creation of an island peasantry. Although they enjoyed some security, these small landholders were never in the early stages entirely free of the necessity for employment. They also found it difficult to adapt to their needs the new cultural patterns which were being pressed upon them without enjoying equal justice and opportunities for advancement. The introduction of indenture labour into Jamaica never became important. The numbers of East Indians entering the island were small; even smaller were the introductions of Europeans, Chinese and Portuguese.

As we have seen, there were many factors which contributed to the difficulties of social integration and development in Jamaica after emancipation. There were old habits for one: the habit of absolute authority on the part of the planter, and the habit of irresponsibility among the labourers. There was also the lessening of the incentive for advancement as the leaders of the emancipation period died out and new opportunities for material gain failed to appear. While neglect of the physical welfare of the labouring population contributed towards its ineffectiveness and hampered its progress; there was the fact that the change of the British sugar market delayed the possible development of social services by forcing the Assembly to cut down on public expenditure; the fact, too, that the ultimate development of the people of Jamaica under freedom could not take place until after slavery had been abolished elsewhere: only then would it become possible for the community to attempt developing the talent and leadership of all sections of the community for mutual advantage.

The road to that development was to lie through the tragedy of Morant Bay, the long slow years of the Crown Colony régime, years saved from complete political stagnation by the work of a few men, and from despair by the encouragement of others; to the events of 1938 and the changes they produced, to the New Constitution of 1944, the rapid advances of 1957 and 1959, to the ultimate achievement of Independence which was to be realised sooner than anyone dared to think.

The driving force behind these developments has been largely political and so the results achieved are most apparent, perhaps, in the political sphere. But the force itself drew its sustenance from something deeper that has grown with the years: from an identification of Jamaicans with Jamaica which finds expression in increasing ways, in art, in literature, in dance, in an interest and new sense of pride in the island's traditions, folklore and history, and in the evidences of that history – the archives, monuments, buildings – as part of a living and continuing process towards still prouder achievements.

The National Dance Theater Company tours regularly throughout the island and abroad

The federal interlude

The years that brought Jamaica the rapid constitutional advances described in Chapter 19, saw also the development of a federation including most of the British West Indian islands.

The idea of grouping these islands for administrative and other purposes was not a new one; attempts had been made almost from the beginning of English settlement. As time went on it had become obvious that the small units (and perhaps even some of the larger ones) could not, individually, support the cost or responsibility of full self-government to which all were moving; but as a united group – a *federation* – this was seen to be possible.

But federation, even of a few units, had not proved popular. The federation of the Leeward Islands in 1871, for example, was accepted unwillingly, while as late as 1936, a proposed union of the Leeward and Windward Islands with Trinidad was described as unlikely to succeed. Poor inter-island communications, insularity fostered by isolation and the tendency of the islands to compete for the same foreign markets and capital, all helped to produce a distrust of each other among West Indians, a distrust which was slow to die. In fact, it was not until after the Second World War that a new attitude to federation began to appear.

Many factors played a part in bringing about the change: better communications between the widely separated territories, for example, and the realisation in time among the leading producers of agricultural products that the islands were no longer competitors. Another important factor was the encouragement given the federal idea by respected West Indian leaders of the period, as well as the support accorded it by several organisations, notably the Barbados Progressive League, the People's National Party and Legislative Council of Jamaica between 1944 and 1945.

By 1945 there were many encouraging signs of growing unity among West Indians, and the British Government made it clear that they proposed to promote federation. The first steps, taken about this time, to set up a university to provide more qualified people for service in the area, was evidence also of Britain's intention to encourage a movement towards independence in the West Indies.

At the suggestion of the Secretary of State for the Colonies a conference to discuss the subject of closer association was held in September 1947 at Montego Bay, attended by delegates from all the territories concerned. At this conference a resolution recognising the need of a political federation was recorded and it was recommended (with the later endorsement of the unit legislatures) that a Standing Closer Association Committee should be set up composed of delegates of legislatures. The report of this Committee, published in 1950, included a provisional scheme for a federal constitution. This scheme formed the basis of the Plan for a British Caribbean Federation which was drawn up at another conference held in London in 1953, and subsequently adopted by the unit legislatures.

The constitution as adopted provided for a Governor-General appointed by the Crown and assisted by a Council of State; the Legislature to consist of two Houses, the Upper House called the Senate, the members of which being nominated by the Governor-General from the various units in the Federation, the Lower House to be elected by full adult suffrage, representation being based on the ten island units making up the Federation as follows: Jamaica 17 seats, Trinidad and Tobago 10, Barbados 5, St Christopher-Nevis-Anguilla, Antigua, Dominica, St Lucia, St Vincent, and Grenada 2 each, and Montserrat 1.

But even at this stage the federal scheme was beset by difficulties. There was suspicion in certain quarters that the larger and stronger units would have to support the smaller and weaker ones, and that federation generally was going to prove too expensive for the West Indies. Freedom of movement among the islands and a customs union of all the islands presented serious problems. Although agreed on the ultimate necessity of both practices, Trinidad (to which other West Indians generally migrated) and Jamaica (which derived a large proportion of its revenue from import duties) were unwilling immediately to shoulder the cost of adopting them. Even more serious, perhaps, was the refusal of the two mainland territories, British Honduras (now Belize) and Guyana, to join the federation.

Nevertheless, the scheme was pursued. Other conferences were held and appointments made to the pre-federal civil service. John (later Sir John) Mordecai, a Jamaican, was appointed Federal Secretary. So the foundations were laid, the structure being shaped at conferences in Barbados, in Jamaica and in Trinidad between October 1956 and January 1958. On 3 January 1958, the Federation formally came into existence; the Right Honourable Lord Hailes, the first Governor-General, took the oath of office at a ceremony in Port-of-Spain where the Federal Capital was situated.

With March set as the time for the election of members to the Federal

The Federation of the West Indies in 1958, and before Independence

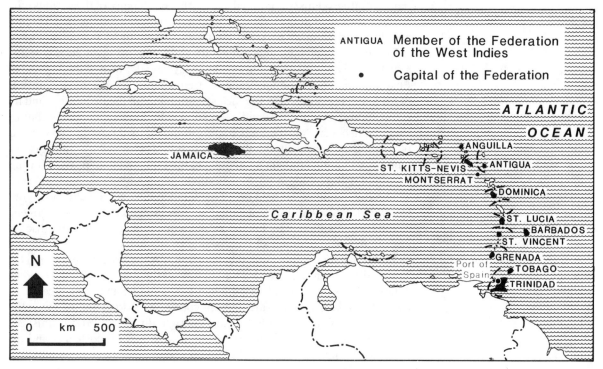

165

Sir (William) Alexander Bustamante, Jamaican statesman and first Prime Minister of a fully independent Jamaica (1962–67).

House of Representatives, political activity on a regional footing began for the first time. Out of this two main parties emerged, the West Indies Federal Labour Party, led by Norman Manley and affiliated with the Jamaica People's National Party, and the Democratic Labour Party of the West Indies, led by Sir Alexander Bustamante in affiliation with his Jamaica Labour Party. The elections took place on 25 March. Although beaten in Jamaica, the W.I.F.L.P. won the majority of seats in the Federal House of Representatives and formed the first Government of the West Indies with Sir Grantley Adams, Premier of Barbados, as first Prime Minister. On 22 April, the first Parliament of the West Indies was formally inaugurated at a ceremony held in the 'Red House', Port-of-Spain, by Her Royal Highness the Princess Margaret, acting on behalf of the Queen.

The ceremony marked what many regarded as the birth of a new nation which, in five years, would take its place as a self-governing dominion within the British Commonwealth. But this was not to be. The experiment in closer association was, in fact, already almost exhausted. Within two years of its inception the Federal Government was being severely criticised by Jamaica and Trinidad. The dispute with Jamaica arose out of the government's decision to grant concessions to an oil company to build and operate an oil refinery in the island. The Federal Prime Minister's threat to counteract such concessions by means of retroactive legislation after 1963 alarmed many Jamaicans. Fearing that federal action of this kind would imperil the country's economic development, Jamaica proposed such changes in the Federal Constitution as would deny the Federal Government powers of direct taxation as well as the power to control the unit economies. Jamaica also demanded an increase in the number of its representatives. This was granted at a stormy conference of the various unit governments held in September 1959 in Trinidad, Jamaica getting 31 seats and Trinidad 15 in an enlarged House consisting of 64 members.

But even these measures failed to prop the now tottering federal structure. The collapse started in May 1960, with Sir Alexander Bustamante's resignation as leader of the Federal D.L.P., the declaration of his party's opposition to Jamaica's continuance in the Federation and its intention to fight for the island's secession. Mr. Manley, declaring that in the circumstances, 'the issue of Federation should, without the intervention of any other issue, come before the people for decision', immediately announced his government's intention to introduce a bill to provide for the taking of a Referendum on the question.

The Referendum was held on 19 September 1961 and resulted in a vote for Jamaica's *withdrawal* from the Federation. The British Government offered no resistance to the island's secession and agreed to discuss immediately the question of its separate statehood.

With Jamaica's withdrawal, the main hope for the Federation centred on Trinidad's continuance in it, but in the early part of 1962, Trinidad announced its intention to withdraw also and to seek independence on its own. Plans were put forward for the continued association of the eight remaining small units, but federation as originally conceived was finished. At midnight of 31 May 1962 it formally went out of existence, and an Interim Commission took over its affairs.

Chapter 21

Independent Jamaica

In Jamaica, the complete acceptance by the government of the result of the Referendum had immediate and far-reaching effects. On the very day following the referendum, the Premier called a meeting of the Cabinet to consider and put in hand the many and varied measures necessary to seek the island's withdrawal from the Federation and its attainment of full independence as early as possible.

Within two weeks a government delegation, led by the Premier, flew to London for discussions with the Secretary of State for the Colonies. These discussions resulted in a large measure of agreement as to the steps necessary for the island's withdrawal from the Federation and achievement of independence on its own.

Back in Jamaica the Premier reported to the House on the results of the London conference and, with the full cooperation of the opposition party, immediately appointed select committees of both Houses of the Legislature to consider and supervise the preparation of a draft Independence Constitution for the island. The reports of these committees were laid before both Houses in January 1962 and, after full debate, unanimously approved.

The proposed constitution was closely based on that already in force. Indeed, the proposals repeated at least eighty per cent of the provisions of the existing instruments. The fact of independence, however, necessitated a number of changes and additions.

It was agreed that Jamaica should seek independence with dominion status within the British Commonwealth of Nations. And, further, that in its basic form the constitution should follow the pattern of the older dominions, as well as some of the more recent, by providing for a Governor-General representing the Queen as the formal depository of the executive authority, with a parliament in whom is vested legal supremacy within the frame of the constitution itself, and a cabinet of ministers controlling the executive of Government and responsible to the Parliament of the Nation.

It was also agreed that the constitution should include provisions covering such matters as citizenship, a Privy Council, the judiciary and a politically-appointed Attorney General, as well as provision for the guarantee of all basic human rights – a provision which may only be amended by large majorities in both Houses of the Legislature, or, failing agreement in the Legislature, by referendum.

On 1 February, independence talks opened at historic Lancaster House in London, between the British Government and a delegation representative of both political parties headed by the Premier and including the Leader of the Opposition. By the 9th the conference had ended, the agreement had been signed, and Jamaica knew the date of its independence – 6 August 1962 – as well as the final form of the constitution with which it would enter into sovereignty. Almost simultaneously the Premier announced that he had fixed 10 April as the date on which a general election would be held to choose the first government for independence.

With only two months to go, the country's political parties (including a newcomer, the People's Political Party) began very active campaigning. This, together with an awareness of the significance of the elections doubtless accounted for the heavy polling on election day. More than seventy-one per cent of the electorate voted, giving the Jamaica Labour Party a decisive majority of 26 seats to the People's National Party's 19. It is believed that the effects of the Referendum had a strong influence on the outcome of the election.

The election over, attention began to turn increasingly towards 6 August and the question of the manner in which the event should be celebrated. A committee, set up by the government in February to prepare a programme of celebrations, had already made good progress. Its activities were to include assistance in the choice of the island's national symbols, the national anthem and flag. It was agreed eventually to retain the three-hundred year old coat-of-arms, but to change the original Latin motto to one in English of greater relevance: 'Out of Many, One People' – a constant reminder of the fact that the Jamaica nation is composed of people of many races who have long lived and worked together in harmony.

The date 30 July marked the beginning of two weeks of celebration and rejoicing such as Jamaica had never witnessed before: and this was fitting, for the celebrations were in honour of the most important event in the country's history.

Independence

These celebrations reached their climax at a solemn but joyous ceremony at midnight on 5 August, at the superb new National Stadium, when the Union Flag of Great Britain was lowered and the island's black, gold and green standard raised for the first time in its place, symbolising the end of British rule and the birth of the *Dominion of Jamaica*. Similar flag-raising ceremonies were also held in parish capitals throughout the island.

On the 7th, (like the 6th it had been declared a public holiday), Her Royal Highness the Princess Margaret, who had arrived in the island four days before to officiate as the Queen's representative, opened the first session of

the first Parliament, read a personal message to the people of Jamaica from Her Majesty and presented to the Prime Minister the Independence Constitutional Instruments. [1] The ceremony was attended by high-ranking ministerial and diplomatic representatives from many countries, including the Vice-President of the United States and other important visitors from abroad, who had been invited to share in the Independence celebrations as guests of the government. Prominent among these guests were three former governors of the island whose administrations, covering the years 1938 to 1957, spanned a crucial period in the country's march to independence.

Sir Kenneth Blackburne, the island's last colonial governor, became with independence the first Governor-General, but his appointment was for a short period: on 1 December 1962 this office, the highest in the land, went to a Jamaican, Sir Clifford Campbell, formerly President of the Senate. On the same day Sir Kenneth left Jamaica on pre-retirement leave.

Four months before a similar break with the past had been ceremonially played out at the Queen's Birthday Parade at Up Park Camp, when the men of the Royal Hampshire Regiment, last of a long line of British troops that had served the country for more than three centuries, marched symbolically through the ranks of the newly-formed Jamaica Regiment, and the Police, and took their leave of the island.

H.R.H. The Princess Margaret opening the first session of Parliament on 7 August, 1962

[1] All these documents are preserved in the Jamaica Archives.

Chapter 22

The last thirty years

Jamaica moved smoothly into its new status as a sovereign state. This was possible because the country had been well prepared for independence with the institutions vital to the process operating efficiently.

Veteran politician that he was, Bustamante stepped easily into the role of director of the island's political affairs. The government's ideological stand was early enunciated by him in his declaration: 'I am for the West. I am against communism.'

There were new government initiatives in a number of areas and by July 1963 a Five-Year Development Plan went to Parliament. It was prepared by Edward Seage, the Minister of Development and Welfare who was to succeed to the prime ministership himself in 1980.

Bustamante retired shortly before the next general election in 1967, when the JLP again won. He was succeeded by Donald Sangster whose sudden death brought Hugh Shearer, a prominent trade unionist, into power as Prime Minister. Meanwhile, Norman Manley, who had retired from active politics at the end of February 1969, died on 2 September of that year.

Bauxite mining and the expansion of industry contributed to the country's growth at this time, but there were serious impediments to the spread of prosperity, notably a rapidly increasing population. Meanwhile, under the leadership of Norman Manley's son Michael (an economist and seasoned trade unionist), the People's National Party, promising social and economic reform, gained ground. In the general election of 1972, it won 37 seats to the JLP's 16.

The promised social change proved to be a move to the left which gained momentum after the party was returned to power in the 1976 election. Close links were established with the USSR and Cuba while relations with the USA deteriorated. Meanwhile, difficulties, aggravated by the drastic increase in world oil prices, brought hardship and consternation, while growing unemployment, severe shortages of even basic necessities, dwindling foreign exchange reserves and successive years of negative growth bred a sense of despair in many quarters.

As the PNP's second term in office drew to its end, the JLP, led now by Edward Seaga, laid down its challenge for leadership. Its main political theme was 'deliverance', especially from what it claimed was economic mismanagement and the threat of an alien political system. In the spring of 1980 Michael Manley announced the calling of early elections. These were held in October and resulted in an overwhelming victory for the Jamaica Labour Party.

In March 1979 the government of Grenada had been taken over in a coup led by Maurice Bishop, and, with Cuban support, transformed into a Marxist-Leninist dictatorship. In October 1983 Bishop and party were ousted, in turn, in a bloody revolution which led to an invasion of that island by the US forces, in which troops from Jamaica participated.

Encouraged, perhaps, by the increase in popularity of the JLP as a result of the island's role in the invasion, Seaga called a snap election. He dissolved Parliament on 28 November, fixed the 29 as Nomination Day, and scheduled elections for 15 December. In this he had acted within his prime ministerial prerogative, but the time allowed for the PNP to prepare for the election was unreasonably short. Claiming that the government had not played by the rules, the People's National Party decided not to contest the elections.

Although excluded from Parliament, the PNP proved to be an influential opposition force, mainly by its ability to mobilise the chief ingredients of an active public opinion.

Meanwhile, as the JLP's second term in office moved to its close, one of the most destructive hurricanes on record struck the island. Its dislocating effects probably delayed the calling of elections at a time when popularity polls showed the JLP surging ahead of the PNP for the first time in years. However, on 7 January 1989 Parliament was dissolved and elections scheduled for a month's time.

In its campaign the Jamaica Labour Party pointed to the achievement of its three main missions during its 8-year term in office – the restoration of peace and stability; economic recovery; and structural adjustment – and asked for a third term in which to bring its 'social well-being programme' to fruition.

On its part the People's National Party, led once more by Michael Manley, stressed this very lack of human resource development during the JLP's eight years in office and promised a government that would 'put people first'. On 9 February Jamaicans went to the polls. The result was a convincing victory for the People's National Party which took 45 of the 60 seats in the country's House of Representatives.

Index

Major references are given in **bold**.
References to footnotes are indicated by 'n', e.g. 128n.